POWER BASICS ®

Earth and Space Science

Robert Taggart

WALCH PUBLISHING

POWER BASICS

Senior Author . . . . Robert Taggart

Editorial Director . . . . Susan Blair

Project Editor . . . . Holly Moirs

Director of Marketing . . . . Jeff Taplin

Senior Production Editor . . . . Maggie Jones

Interior Design . . . . Mark Sayer

Cover Design . . . . Roman Laszok

Typesetting . . . . Sheila Russell
Mark Sayer
Ian Weidner

Editorial Staff . . . . Elizabeth Lynch
Richard Lynch
Kate O'Halloran
Mary Rich
Erica Varney

3   4   5   6   7   8   9   10

ISBN 0-8251-5634-3

Copyright © 1998, 2001, 2005

J. Weston Walch, Publisher

P. O. Box 658 • Portland, Maine 04104-0658

walch.com

Printed in the United States of America

WALCH PUBLISHING

Table of Contents

To the Student

Welcome to *Power Basics® Earth and Space Science,* a course designed to help you understand the planet we call home.

Unit 1: The Universe Around Us teaches about the universe from the moment it was created between 12 and 15 billion years ago. You will learn about stars, galaxies, and planets. You will also learn about Earth and its solar system.

In **Unit 2: The Atmosphere Around Us,** you will learn about Earth's atmosphere, weather and winds, and climate.

Unit 3: The Ground Beneath Us teaches about Earth's structure and about the minerals, rocks, and fossil fuels that can be found within Earth's outer layer. You will also become familiar with the theory of plate tectonics, the history of Earth, and ways to measure and map the globe.

In **Unit 4: Earth's Water Systems,** you will learn why Earth is called the "water planet," and how water has always been an important life-giving and ground-shaping force. You will also study Earth's oceans, rivers, glaciers, and groundwater.

There are four lessons in each part of this book. Each lesson includes many things to help you learn. "Tips" will give you hints on how to make learning easier. "In Real Life" sections will show you how the skills you are learning apply to the world around you. "Think About It" questions will ask you to think about Earth in new ways.

You may find some unfamiliar or difficult scientific terms in this book. If you need to know the meaning or pronunciation of a word or a group of words, remember that you can look in the glossary for this information. Your teacher or instructor can also help.

We hope you will use *Power Basics Earth and Space Science* to master skills that will help you understand and appreciate the world around you. And, we hope you will enjoy yourself as you learn!

UNIT 1

The Universe Around Us

LESSON 1: The Cosmos

GOAL: To understand the four areas of earth science; to understand the formation of our universe

WORDS TO KNOW

absolute magnitude	meteorology
apparent magnitude	nuclear fusion
astronomy	oceanography
Big Bang	orbit
binary stars	pulsar
black hole	quasars
Cepheid variables	radio telescopes
cosmologists	red giant
earth science	redshift
El Niño	reflecting telescope
electromagnetic spectrum	refracting telescope
elliptical galaxies	speed of light
galaxies	spiral galaxies
geology	stars
gravity	supernova
irregular galaxies	telescope
light-year	wave
Local Group	white dwarf

What Is Earth Science?

Do you realize that you are living on a spaceship? Planet Earth is a spaceship complete with its own life-support system. Spaceship Earth orbits the Sun, while the Sun orbits the center of the Milky Way Galaxy, which itself is whirling through space. It is easy to forget that your home, planet Earth, is just a tiny part of the endless cosmos.

The construction of spaceship Earth began 4.6 billion years ago, and Earth has been changing ever since. From a single grain of sand washing away to lava building up the land, Earth changes a little bit every day.

Earth science is the study of the systems and cycles that keep Earth both changing and constant. There are four areas of earth science: **geology, astronomy, meteorology,** and **oceanography.**

Geology

When the volcano Mauna Loa erupts in Hawaii, it sends lava flowing over land and releases gases into the atmosphere. The study of how volcanoes are formed and what happens when they erupt is part of geology. Geology is the study of Earth's surface and its interior. A person who studies geology is called a geologist. A geologist studies events such as volcanic eruptions and earthquakes.

Astronomy

When a meteorite falls from the sky, it delivers its own mixture of minerals and elements to Earth's landscape. The study of meteorites is part of astronomy. Astronomy is the study of the universe. A person who studies astronomy is called an astronomer. An astronomer studies events such as the nuclear fusions that take place in the Sun and the motion of the planets that orbit it.

TIP

Earth **orbits,** or circles around, the Sun. The word *orbit* also means the path that an object takes. Earth's orbit around the Sun is shaped like an ellipse.

Meteorology

When **El Niño** (a warm ocean current) arrives, it brings heavy winds, rains, floods, and mudslides to California. This warm water current is a result of Earth's prevailing winds. The study of El Niño and its effect on Earth's weather is part of meteorology. Meteorology is the study of Earth's atmosphere and weather. A person who studies meteorology is called a meteorologist. A meteorologist studies events like powerful, unpredictable weather systems and the endless, steady passage of water through the water cycle.

Oceanography

The study of El Niño overlaps into another area of earth science. El Niño's effect on Earth's oceans is part of oceanography. Oceanography is the study of Earth's oceans. A person who studies oceanography is called an oceanographer. An oceanographer studies events such as crashing waves eroding a beach and the steady ocean currents that follow the same path year after year.

■ PRACTICE 1: What Is Earth Science?

Decide if each event that follows is part of geology (**G**), astronomy (**A**), meteorology (**M**), or oceanography (**O**). Write the correct letter on each line.

_____ **1.** Earth's orbit around the Sun

_____ **2.** a hurricane in New England

_____ **3.** a volcanic eruption in Hawaii

_____ **4.** ocean waves

_____ **5.** a flood in Arkansas

_____ **6.** a blizzard in Michigan

_____ **7.** an earthquake in San Francisco

What Is Light?

Your view of the cosmos from Earth depends on the light that reaches your eyes. You probably know that sound travels in **waves.** Did you know that light also travels in waves? What you call light is actually an electromagnetic wave. There are other types of electromagnetic waves that are probably familiar to you, such as X rays, radio waves, gamma rays, and microwaves. All electromagnetic waves carry energy. Gamma rays and X rays carry a high amount of energy. They can penetrate through thick layers of most materials. Radio waves and microwaves carry less energy and are less penetrating. The total range of all electromagnetic waves is shown on the **electromagnetic spectrum.** Unlike the other waves found on the electromagnetic spectrum, light waves are visible to us.

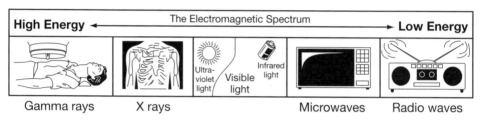

Types of Electromagnetic Waves

All electromagnetic waves have two things in common. First, all electromagnetic waves travel at the **speed of light**—300,000 kilometers each second. Second, as they travel, all electromagnetic waves carry energy, just like ocean waves and sound waves do. When you turn on a lamp, electromagnetic waves carry energy in the form of light outward from the lightbulb. The light reaches your eyes so quickly you do not notice any delay. If the lamp were directed out into space, the light would be 300,000 kilometers away from Earth after just one second. After one year, the light from your lamp would have traveled 9.4 trillion kilometers! The distance that light can travel in one year is known as a **light-year.**

TIP

Do not confuse radio waves with sound waves. The only way sound waves can travel is through matter. Since there is no air in space, sound waves cannot travel through space. Like all electromagnetic waves, radio waves can travel through air and space.

A light-year is a convenient measure of distance in the vast universe. The closest star to Earth, other than the Sun, is Proxima Centauri. Proxima Centauri is 4.2 light-years away. When you look at Proxima Centauri, you are seeing the light that left it 4.2 years ago. Looking at the stars is more than just looking at points of light in the sky. It is like looking into the past. The night sky offers many clues to the origin of the universe.

Telescopes

Since 1610, when Italian astronomer Galileo first pointed a telescope to the sky, telescopes have been an essential (necessary) tool of the astronomer. A **telescope** is a tool used to view distant objects. A telescope that gathers light waves is called an optical telescope. Some optical telescopes, like Galileo's, use curved pieces of glass, called lenses, to collect and focus light. This type of telescope is called a **refracting telescope.** Another type of telescope, called a **reflecting telescope,** uses curved mirrors. Today's telescopes can not only collect light, but they can store it on film or in a computer. Because a telescope can be directed at an object for many hours, it can detect far more about the sky than a person's eyes alone can.

The amount of light that a telescope can gather depends on the diameter of its lens or mirror. The larger the diameter, the more light the telescope collects. The largest optical telescope on Earth is the Keck Telescope in Hawaii. Its mirror is almost 10 meters in diameter. In space, the Hubble Space Telescope orbits more than 600 kilometers above Earth's surface. There, light reaches the Hubble's 2.4-meter mirror before it passes through the atmosphere. Since 1993, the Hubble Space Telescope has sent spectacular photographs of space objects to Earth.

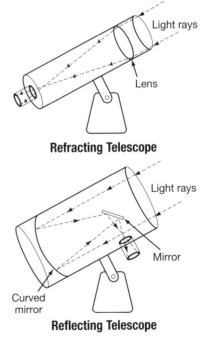

Refracting Telescope

Reflecting Telescope

When you see stars twinkling at night, the twinkling is not the star, but an effect of Earth's atmosphere. Starlight passing through the atmosphere is bent and distorted, making stars appear to twinkle. Twinkling stars may look pretty, but they are an annoying problem to astronomers. The distortion of light makes it hard for astronomers to get a clear and focused image of the star.

Some space objects send out more than just light waves. X rays, gamma rays, ultraviolet waves, infrared waves, and radio waves have also been detected. **Radio telescopes** gather energy in the form of radio waves from deep space objects. Radio telescopes have large curved dishes. Astronomers also use radio telescopes to search for signals sent by extra-terrestrial (from some place other than Earth) beings. So far, no signals have been detected.

■ PRACTICE 2: What Is Light?

Decide if each statement that follows is true (**T**) or false (**F**). Write the correct letter on each line.

_____ **1.** Light is an electromagnetic wave.

_____ **2.** All waves on the electromagnetic spectrum are visible waves.

_____ **3.** The speed of light is also the speed of radio waves.

_____ **4.** A light-year is the distance that light can travel in one year.

_____ **5.** In a way, looking at the stars is like looking into the past.

_____ **6.** A refracting telescope uses mirrors.

_____ **7.** The Hubble Space Telescope is the largest telescope on the ground.

_____ **8.** Radio telescopes gather energy in the form of radio waves.

The Big Bang Theory

The construction of Earth that began 4.6 billion years ago is only part of the history of the much larger universe. How did the universe begin? Those who study the origin and structure of the universe are called **cosmologists.** Cosmologists look to outer space for their answers.

In 1929, astronomer and cosmologist Edwin Hubble used a telescope to measure light coming from systems of stars called **galaxies.** His measurements showed a shift in the spectrum of light coming from there. This shift in light showed that the galaxies were moving away from Earth and away from one another. This shift in light is called **redshift.** Hubble concluded that the universe was expanding. The Hubble Space Telescope was named in honor of Edwin Hubble.

Hubble's work led others to propose the **Big Bang** theory. The Big Bang theory states that the universe began with a giant explosion between 12 and 15 billion years ago. In the moments after it was created, the universe was what cosmologists call a primordial soup—a mixture of subatomic particles and radiation all rushing about at temperatures over 10 billion degrees Celsius. After three minutes, the soup had cooled enough for the first bits of matter to form.

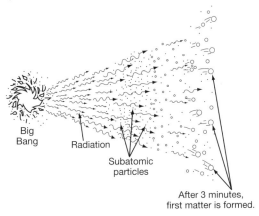

Big Bang

Radiation

Subatomic particles

After 3 minutes, first matter is formed.

Big Bang Theory

The matter that formed in those first moments became the building blocks for all matter in the universe. Everything around you today is made of particles that were created between 12 and 15 billion years ago in the Big Bang.

Today, most cosmologists accept the Big Bang theory. Their view of the universe is of a vast space with no center or edges. These scientists believe that the universe is governed by the same laws of nature found on Earth.

Today, many cosmologists wonder whether the universe will expand forever or eventually collapse. The key to answering this question lies in estimating the amount of matter there is in the universe. All matter is affected by **gravity.** The law of gravity states that all of the matter in the universe is attracted toward other matter. Gravity is the force that holds you to Earth's surface. If there is enough matter in the universe, the force of gravity might eventually stop the expansion. Then, the universe would begin a slow collapse. The collapse would end in what cosmologists are now calling the Big Crunch.

TIP

To imagine an expanding universe, think of a loaf of raisin bread rising as it bakes. The raisins are like the galaxies moving away from one another as the loaf expands.

■ PRACTICE 3: The Big Bang Theory

Decide if each statement that follows is true (**T**) or false (**F**). Write the correct letter on each line.

_____ **1.** Cosmologists study the origin and structure of the universe.

_____ **2.** Edwin Hubble noticed a redshift in light from the galaxies.

_____ **3.** The universe is collapsing.

_____ **4.** The Big Crunch states that the universe began with an explosion.

_____ **5.** The first bits of matter were created three minutes after the Big Bang.

_____ **6.** If there is enough matter in the universe, it might continue expanding.

Galaxies

Galaxies are systems of stars. You live in a galaxy called the Milky Way Galaxy. The Sun is just one of billions of stars in the Milky Way Galaxy. The Milky Way Galaxy is just one of billions of galaxies that astronomers have observed. When astronomers look out through the great distances of the universe, they are looking back through time at what the universe was like when it was young. In this way, they can piece together how galaxies formed.

Young galaxies began to form in the first few million years after the Big Bang. They are now very old. Gravity pulled together enormous clouds of gas and dust. In the oldest and most distant galaxies that can be seen, astronomers find quasars. **Quasars** are like stars, except they give off strong radio signals. Quasars are believed to be the visible centers of distant galaxies. Quasars throw out more energy than any other object in the sky. In the very center of a quasar is believed to be a black hole. A **black hole** is a dense region with gravity so strong that it swallows up all matter around it. No light or other electromagnetic waves can escape from a black hole. Quasars are like super hot whirlpools where gas and stars are sucked into the black hole center.

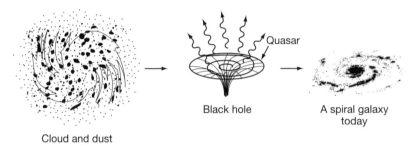

Cloud and dust

Black hole

Quasar

A spiral galaxy today

Galaxy Formation

Since quasars are only seen in the most distant and, therefore, oldest galaxies, astronomers believe that quasars eventually died out. The light that we see from quasars took so long to reach us that although the quasar is gone, we can still see light from it. Yet, astronomers think that younger galaxies, including the Milky Way, still have a black hole at their centers.

There are three types of galaxies.

Spiral Galaxies

Spiral galaxies, such as the Milky Way Galaxy, contain gas and dust from which new stars are being made. Seen from above, a spiral galaxy has spiral arms and is shaped like a pinwheel. Seen from the edge, a spiral galaxy is a thin disk with a bulging center where the concentration of stars is the greatest. The Milky Way Galaxy is 120,000 light-years across. The Sun is within one of the spiral arms of the Milky Way Galaxy—about 30,000 light-years from the center. Earth, along with the Sun and billions of other stars, slowly revolves around the galaxy's center, which may contain a black hole.

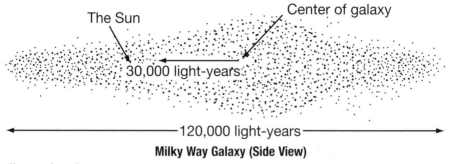

Milky Way Galaxy (Side View)

Elliptical Galaxies

Elliptical galaxies are shaped like a round ball or an oval. More than half of all galaxies are elliptical. Since elliptical galaxies have very little gas and dust, no new stars are made.

Irregular Galaxies

Irregular galaxies have no definite shape. A small percentage of galaxies are irregular.

Galaxies of all kinds are found in clusters throughout the universe. The Milky Way Galaxy belongs to a cluster of galaxies called the **Local Group**. The Andromeda Galaxy is another spiral galaxy in the Local Group. It is over 2 million light-years away, but it can be seen from Earth without the aid of a telescope. It allows all of us to observe a galaxy much like our own.

IN REAL LIFE

Long before they knew it was a galaxy, observers of the night sky named the hazy, glowing band that stretches across the night sky the Milky Way. You might have seen the Milky Way on a clear night.

■ PRACTICE 4: Galaxies

Decide if each statement that follows is true (**T**) or false (**F**). Write the correct letter on each line.

_____ **1.** The Sun is part of a system of stars called the Milky Way Galaxy.

_____ **2.** Quasars are at the center of very old galaxies.

_____ **3.** Astronomers think that there are black holes at the center of galaxies.

_____ **4.** Galaxies shaped like a pinwheel are called spiral galaxies.

_____ **5.** Most of the galaxies in the universe are irregular galaxies.

_____ **6.** The Andromeda Galaxy and the Milky Way Galaxy are part of a cluster of galaxies called the Local Group.

The Stars

Stars are giant balls of burning gas. The first stars were created during the first few million years after the Big Bang—at the same time the galaxies were forming. Stars began as clouds of hydrogen gas within the still young galaxies. As gravity pulled the clouds of gas together, a dense, hot core was formed. Temperatures soared in the core. Atoms of hydrogen smashed into one another. When the temperature was correct, the particles began pushing into one another, or fusing, to make helium. This process of fusing hydrogen into helium is called **nuclear fusion.** Nuclear fusion is what made stars start to glow.

Nuclear fusion creates huge amounts of light energy. For millions of years after the Big Bang, the universe was dark. After stars were born, the universe began to glow. Since that time, many new stars have been born, and many stars have died. What is the expected lifetime of a star? It depends on the star's mass. Large, massive stars burn their hydrogen at a higher rate than smaller stars. As a result, large stars burn out faster than small stars.

The Sun is an average-sized star that was born only 5 billion years

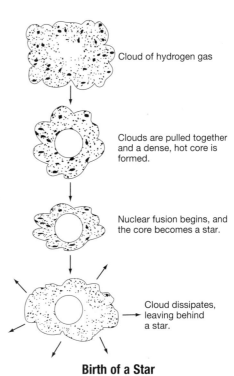

Cloud of hydrogen gas

Clouds are pulled together and a dense, hot core is formed.

Nuclear fusion begins, and the core becomes a star.

Cloud dissipates, leaving behind a star.

Birth of a Star

ago. In another 5 billion years, the hydrogen supply in its core will be used up. At that point, gravity will begin to take over, and the Sun will begin its slow death. As the core of the Sun collapses, temperatures within it will rise. Heat from the core will make the outer shell of the star expand for a time. Any remaining hydrogen in the shell will burn up. The Sun will have become a **red giant.** At this stage, spaceship Earth will be baked to a crisp. When all of the hydrogen in the Sun is finally burned, the Sun will completely collapse into a **white dwarf.**

Large, massive stars use up their hydrogen supply after only 10 million years. When fusion stops, a large star becomes a red supergiant. When a red supergiant starts to collapse, there is a huge sudden

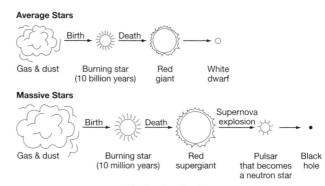

Life Cycle of a Star

explosion called a **supernova.** All but the core of the star is blown outward into space. What is left of the core becomes a very dense pulsar. A **pulsar** sends out radio waves in pulses. Another word for a pulsar is a neutron star. Even more massive stars continue collapsing until their gravitational pull is much stronger. At some point, the gravity is stronger than the escape velocity of light, and the object is called a black hole. Nothing can escape from a black hole, not even light.

The Big Bang only created the elements hydrogen and helium. The rest of the elements were created in nuclear reactions that take place in large stars. Supernovas spread such elements far out into space. Except for hydrogen and helium, all the elements that exist in the universe, on planet Earth, and in you were created in the fusion process of large stars.

Different Kinds of Stars

Except for a brilliant supernova in a distant galaxy, all the stars seen in the sky are in the Milky Way Galaxy. Most of these stars are in their hydrogen-burning stage, like the Sun. There is a special class of stars called the **Cepheid variables.** These stars get brighter or dimmer at regular intervals of time. Astronomers have been able to use the pulse rate of a Cepheid variable to determine its distance from Earth. **Binary stars** are also of special interest to astronomers. Binary stars are two stars that revolve around each other. The time it takes for them to revolve helps astronomers calculate their size, mass, and density.

Star Brightness

When you look at the stars in the sky, most of them seem to be white dots. But, if you look closely, you will see that others appear to be slightly red or slightly blue. The color of a star is an indication of how hot the star is burning. Blue-white stars are the hottest and brightest. Yellow stars, like the Sun, are medium hot. Red stars are the coolest and dimmest.

The measure of how bright a star appears is called its **apparent magnitude.** Apparent magnitude does not represent the star's true brightness, because each star is located a different distance from Earth. **Absolute magnitude** is a measure of how bright stars would really be if they were all compared at the same distance (32.6 light-years). The brightest stars have a lower magnitude number. In fact, some stars are so bright they have a negative number for magnitude.

Star	Distance from Earth	Apparent Magnitude	Absolute Magnitude	Color
Sun	8 light-minutes	−26.8	4.85	Yellow
Sirius	8.7 light-years	−1.47	1.4	Blue
Betelgeuse	520 light-years	.41	−5.6	Red

The Sun is actually a dim star. Sirius, the brightest star seen in the nighttime sky, does not have the greatest absolute magnitude. It appears to be brighter because it is closer to us. Betelgeuse is 520 light-years from Earth. It greatly outshines Sirius in absolute magnitude.

■ PRACTICE 5: The Stars

Circle the answer that correctly completes each of the following statements.

1. The first stars began to glow _____.
   a. minutes after the Big Bang
   b. when nuclear fusion began in the core
   c. both *a* and *b*

2. Compared to a smaller star, a large, heavy star will burn _____.
   a. at the same rate
   b. much longer
   c. more quickly

3. A star that dies by expanding into a red giant, then collapsing into a white dwarf is _____.
   a. a small star
   b. a large, heavy star
   c. an average-sized star

4. Supernovas _____.
   a. are explosions of large stars
   b. are the cores of neutron stars
   c. are black holes

5. Two stars that revolve around each other are called _____.
   a. pulsars
   b. binary stars
   c. Cepheid variables

6. The measure of how bright a star really is, is called _____.
   a. absolute magnitude
   b. apparent magnitude
   c. star color

LESSON 2: The Solar System

GOAL: To understand the origins and motions of the parts of the solar system

WORDS TO KNOW

asteroids	maxima	revolves
aurora	meteor	rings
chromosphere	meteorite	rotates
comets	meteoroids	solar flares
convective zone	minima	solar prominences
corona	Oort cloud	solar wind
Galilean moons	orbital period	sunspots
Great Red Spot	photosphere	terrestrial
Jovian	radiative zone	

The Sun

Between 7 and 10 billion years after the Big Bang, a star was born in one of the spiral arms of a galaxy. Surrounding the star were clumps of gas and rock. The clumps were too small to ever turn into stars. They circled around the star, becoming more and more compact. Today, 5 billion years later, that star is the Sun, and the clumps of gas and rock have become the planets, moons, asteroids, meteoroids, and comets that make up the solar system.

The Sun is a ball of burning gas 1.4 million kilometers in diameter. Its average distance from Earth is 149,600,000 kilometers. The Sun's main source of fuel is hydrogen. Nuclear fusion takes place in the core (center) of the Sun. In the process of changing hydrogen into helium, some of the matter is changed directly into energy. Nuclear fusion in the core is the source of the Sun's tremendous energy.

The nuclear energy produced by the Sun seeps outward from its core. The energy, in the form of invisible X rays and gamma rays, radiates through a region known as the **radiative zone** that surrounds the core. As the energy travels outward, it passes through a layer called the **convective zone.** In the convective zone, gases boil and rise in huge convection currents. The convection currents carry the energy of the Sun to its outer layer in the form of light waves. The outer layer of the Sun is called the photosphere. The surface of the **photosphere** is grainy because of the boiling gases beneath it. You see the photosphere when you look toward the Sun. (Always be careful not to look directly at the Sun. Direct rays can injure your eyes.)

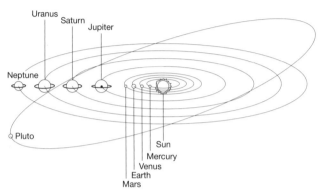

The Solar System

Just like Earth, the Sun has an atmosphere. Normally you cannot see the atmosphere because it is hidden in the glare of the Sun's disk. Astronomers get their best views of the Sun's atmosphere when the disk is covered. This happens naturally during a total solar eclipse, when the Moon just covers the disk of the Sun.

There are two layers in the Sun's atmosphere. The **chromosphere** is a thin layer of gases surrounding the Sun. The chromosphere has a pinkish-red glow. Outside of the chromosphere is the huge outer atmosphere of the Sun called the **corona.** The corona is made of thin, hot gases that stretch

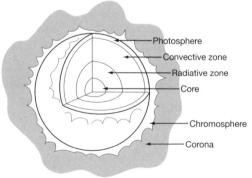

The Structure of the Sun

for millions of kilometers into space. During an eclipse, the corona looks like a thin halo or crown surrounding the Sun.

TIP

The word *photo* means light. The photosphere is the layer that radiates light. The word *corona* means crown. The corona is like a crown surrounding the Sun.

The Sun is a magnet, just like Earth. It has a north pole and a south pole. Sometimes, giant magnetic storms erupt on the surface of the Sun. Viewed from Earth, these storms appear as dark spots on the Sun's surface. These spots are called **sunspots.** Sunspots are dark because they are cooler than the surrounding Sun. Sunspots move across the surface of the Sun as it rotates. The number of sunspots changes in cycles of 11 years. During sunspot **minima,** there is little magnetic activity on the Sun. During sunspot **maxima,** the Sun's magnetic activity reaches a peak.

Solar flares are explosions from sunspots that send waves of energy into space. When the energy reaches Earth, it can black out communication networks and make magnetic compasses spin. Solar flares can interact with Earth's magnetic field and cause an eerie light show, called an **aurora,** near the poles. In the Northern Hemisphere, this light show is called the Aurora Borealis. In the Southern Hemisphere, it is called the Aurora Australis. **Solar prominences** are also caused by the magnetic forces in the Sun. Prominences are huge loops, or arches of cooler gas, that rise through the corona. They can last for several hours or up to several weeks.

A great many charged particles fly out from the Sun at all times. The outburst of particles increases during sunspot maxima. These particles stream outward on the **solar wind.** Earth is protected, for the most part, from the onslaught of charged particles by its own magnetic field. This

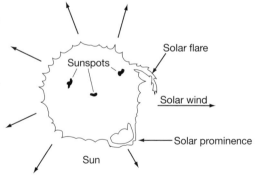

magnetic field acts like a shield. The particles in the solar wind flow around Earth and continue through the solar system.

The Sun is at the center of the solar system. On Earth, we have always recognized the importance of the Sun. It is our single most important source of life and energy. Plants depend on it for food through the process of photosynthesis. Energy from the Sun is the foundation of the food chain. The Sun's heating of the atmosphere keeps us warm, produces winds, and brings rain. The Sun is indirectly a source of natural gas, coal, and oil. You might say that the Sun is the "star" of our solar system!

■ PRACTICE 6: The Sun

Decide if each statement that follows is true (**T**) or false (**F**). Write the correct letter on each line.

_____ 1. Nuclear fusion in the Sun's core changes some matter directly into energy.

_____ 2. In the Sun, X rays radiate through the convective zone.

_____ 3. The photosphere is part of the Sun's atmosphere.

_____ 4. The Sun's corona is smaller than the chromosphere.

_____ 5. Sunspots are hotter than the surrounding Sun.

_____ 6. Solar flares are explosions from sunspots.

_____ 7. The solar wind carries a stream of charged particles.

Terrestrial Planets

Earth, the third planet from the Sun, is one of the five **terrestrial** planets in the solar system. Terrestrial means "of Earth." The four other terrestrial planets—Mercury, Venus, Mars, and Pluto—are made of rock just like Earth. Most terrestrial planets are also called the inner planets because they are closest to the Sun in the inner part of the solar system. Except for

Pluto, you can see each of the terrestrial planets without the aid of a telescope. (See Appendix A on p. 213 for more information.)

Five billion years ago, when the Sun was born, the remaining gas and rocks were sorted naturally. Only the rocky materials could survive closest to the Sun's heat. Farther away from the Sun, where it was cooler, gases collected. By 4.6 billion years ago, the rocky materials had grouped together to become the terrestrial planets. In the outer solar system, the large gas planets, Jupiter, Saturn, Uranus, and Neptune, had formed. For the first few million years, the terrestrial planets were wild places. Volcanic eruptions released heat and molten rock. Bits of rock and debris bombarded the inner planets, leaving huge pockmarks called impact craters.

Mercury

Mercury is the planet closest to the Sun. Like all the planets, Mercury **revolves** around, or circles, the Sun in a slightly elliptical (oval-shaped) orbit. A year on Mercury—or the time it takes the planet to revolve once around the Sun—is 88 days. Like the other planets, Mercury also **rotates,** or spins, on an axis. A day on Mercury—or the time it takes the planet to complete one rotation—lasts 59 Earth-days. As a result of its long day and closeness to the Sun, temperatures can reach 427°C. During the long night, temperatures drop to −185°C.

In 1974, *Mariner 10,* an unmanned spacecraft, flew by Mercury and returned the first photographs of its surface. The photographs showed that Mercury is covered with impact craters. Between craters are fields of lava made in volcanoes. Gravity on Mercury is only $\frac{2}{5}$ the gravity on Earth. The weak gravity cannot hold an atmosphere to the planet's surface. Thus, like the Moon, the impact craters remain intact since there is no wind or rain to wash them away. If you could fly by Mercury, you would find

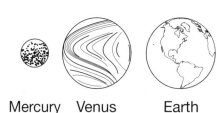

Mercury   Venus   Earth   Mars

Inner Terrestrial Planets

a dry, hot, airless, completely silent planet with a huge Sun that appears to move very slowly across a black sky.

Venus

Venus is the second of the inner planets. You have probably seen Venus shining brightly in the sky around sunrise or sunset. To see both Mercury and Venus, you must look toward the Sun, since they are both closer to the Sun than Earth is. Venus is easier to see since it is bigger than Mercury and not as close to the Sun.

THINK ABOUT IT

Since they are seen only at sunrise and sunset, Venus and Mercury are often called "evening stars" or "morning stars." What is wrong with that description? Write your answer on a separate sheet of paper.

Venus is a beautiful sight to behold. But Venus is not a beautiful place to visit. Venus is called Earth's sister planet, since it is about the same size and mass as Earth. However, Venus is completely covered in a thick atmosphere of carbon dioxide with poisonous clouds of sulfuric acid. The thick atmosphere traps heat. Temperatures on Venus top 500°C all the time. Venus has other strange properties. Because Venus rotates slower than it revolves, a "day" lasts 18 Earth days longer than a "year" on Venus. Venus rotates in the opposite direction of all the other planets, except Pluto and Uranus. The Sun, if you could see it, rises in the west and sets in the east over a surface of volcanic rock.

Mars

Mars is the fourth planet from the Sun and the first planet outside of Earth's orbit. The surface of Mars is red from rusted iron in the soil. Mars' thin atmosphere cannot trap heat, so Mars, with an average temperature below freezing, is colder than Earth. Huge duststorms are stirred up by winds that sweep the surface. Mars has two tiny, irregularly shaped moons, Phobos and Deimos.

Mars and Earth have similarities. A Martian day is just a little longer than an Earth day. Since its axis is tilted the same as Earth's, Mars has seasons. As on Earth, there is water on Mars. Water is in the atmosphere and is frozen in the ice caps that cover the North and South Poles. Ancient, dried-up riverbeds and seabeds indicate that water used to run over the surface. Where is the water now? Astronomers think that most of the water is frozen underground.

Evidence suggests that there was once life on Mars. Scientists believe that a meteorite found in Antarctica is a Martian rock. Scientists analyzed the rock and found evidence of tiny bacteria that may have lived on Mars 3.6 billion years ago. Is there life on Mars now? Only future exploration will tell.

Pluto

Pluto is the smallest, coldest, most distant planet known. It is a tiny terrestrial planet. Pluto's orbit is highly elliptical and is tilted compared to the plane of orbit of the other planets. Sometimes its orbit crosses Neptune's. When this happens, Pluto is really the eighth planet from the Sun. No spacecraft has flown by Pluto. However, the Hubble Space Telescope has shown that Pluto has blotchy regions of light and dark on its surface. The light regions may be lighter-colored highlands or areas covered with frost. Pluto has a small moon called Charon.

■ PRACTICE 7: Terrestrial Planets

Look at the list of planets below. Fill in each line with the letter of the planet that correctly fits each description. (*Hint:* Some descriptions have more than one answer.)

a. Mercury   **b.** Venus   **c.** Earth   **d.** Mars   **e.** Pluto

_____ **1.** closest to the Sun

_____ **2.** thick atmosphere

_____ **3.** impact craters still intact

_____ **4.** dried-up riverbeds

_____ **5.** sunrise in the west

_____ **6.** evidence of life long ago

_____ **7.** made of rock

_____ **8.** planet with the most elliptical orbit

_____ **9.** seen without a telescope

_____ **10.** has a moon (or two)

_____ **11.** has seasons

_____ **12.** morning or evening "stars"

_____ **13.** red surface

_____ **14.** dry, hot, and airless

_____ **15.** definite signs of life

_____ **16.** the smallest, coldest planet

The Jovian Planets

The outer planets, except for Pluto, are known as the Jovian planets. Jovian
means that the planets are all similar to Jupiter. Jupiter, Saturn, Uranus,
and Neptune are much larger than the terrestrial planets. Each Jovian
planet is thought to have a core of rock surrounded by a liquid layer. The
outer layer is mainly hydrogen and helium gas. All of the Jovian planets
have ring systems made of tiny orbiting particles called **rings.** Saturn is the
planet best known for its rings.

THINK ABOUT IT

The length of a planet's year is determined by its distance from the Sun. Using the information from the table on page 214, complete the following sentence: The farther a planet is from the Sun, the _____ the year. Can you make a similar statement about the length of day? Write your answer on a separate sheet of paper.

Jupiter

Jupiter, the fifth planet from the Sun, is the largest planet in the solar system. Jupiter spins rapidly, completing a "day" in just under 10 hours. Jupiter has an extremely hot core. It delivers twice as much heat back to space as it receives from the Sun. The heat and rapid rotation of the planet create a pattern of swirling bands across the surface.

On Jupiter's surface is a giant storm, larger than Earth, called the **Great Red Spot.** This storm drifts across the planet but always stays below the equator. (An equator is the imaginary line that cuts any sphere in half.) The Great Red Spot is a mystery that astronomers are still trying to figure out.

With over 60 moons, Jupiter is the center of its own mini "solar" system. In 1610, Galileo pointed his telescope at Jupiter and discovered its four largest moons, now called the **Galilean moons.** The *Voyager* mission, launched in 1979, provided information about the Galilean moons.

Io, the innermost of the Galilean moons, has the most volcanic activity of all the planets and moons in the solar system. No impact craters remain on its orange and red surface. Europa is the next closest to Jupiter. It is the smallest of the Galilean moons. Europa is the smoothest object in the solar system. It has an icy crust that is crisscrossed with dark cracks.

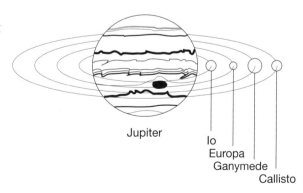

Jupiter

Io
Europa
Ganymede
Callisto

Ganymede is the third and largest of the Galilean moons. It is nearly as big as Mars. Ganymede has a wrinkled, icy surface speckled with impact craters. Callisto is the outermost Galilean moon. Callisto is covered with impact craters made in the early days of the solar system. It is the only Galilean moon whose impact craters have not been covered with ice or lava.

Saturn

The most striking feature of the sixth planet is its beautiful ring system. Saturn's rings are made of billions of icy particles that are arranged in flat planes extending 72,000 kilometers into space. Saturn is similar to Jupiter. It is large, rotates rapidly, is covered in colored bands of gas, and delivers more heat to space than it gets from the Sun. Saturn also has its own mini "solar" system, with at least 34 moons. The largest and most interesting of Saturn's moons is Titan. Titan is larger than Mercury and is the only moon in the solar system with a thick atmosphere.

Uranus

Uranus is the seventh planet. Unlike Jupiter and Saturn, Uranus appears completely smooth. Its color is a beautiful blue-green. This color comes from methane gas in its atmosphere. Uranus is unusual because it orbits the Sun tilted on its side, rolling along like a spinning top. Uranus has at least 27 moons. Ten of them were discovered when the *Voyager* mission flew by. Astronomers discovered additional moons using the Hubble Space Telescope.

Neptune

Neptune is the most distant of the Jovian planets. The small amount of sunlight reaching Neptune makes it too dim to be seen without the help of a telescope. Neptune is blue-green like Uranus, but not as smooth. *Voyager* visited Neptune and discovered that it has an active, banded atmosphere, like Jupiter's. It has a Great Dark Spot that is not a storm, but a hole in the clouds. Triton, the largest of Neptune's eight known moons, has active geysers that spew out water and nitrogen.

■ PRACTICE 8: The Jovian Planets

Look at the list of terms below. Fill in each line with the letter of the term that correctly identifies each description. (*Hint:* More than one answer may be correct.)

_____ 1. delivers more heat than it gets

_____ 2. has a blue-green color

_____ 3. has ring systems

_____ 4. most volcanic body in the solar system

_____ 5. where the Great Red Spot is found

_____ 6. has at least 27 moons

_____ 7. tilts on its side

_____ 8. has a Great Dark Spot

_____ 9. largest moon of Saturn

_____ 10. largest moon of Neptune

a. Jupiter

b. Saturn

c. Uranus

d. Neptune

e. Io

f. Europa

g. Ganymede

h. Callisto

i. Titan

j. Triton

Comets, Meteoroids, and Asteroids

Comets

Many objects other than the planets and their moons belong to the Sun's family. The most spectacular are comets. Comets were described as "dirty snowballs" by astronomer Fred Whipple in 1950. Comets are nothing more than chunks of ice and dust. They move

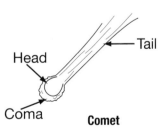

27

in highly elliptical orbits around the Sun. A comet's **orbital period**—the time it takes to orbit the Sun—can be as few as 3 years and as long as 80,000 years. During most of its orbital period, the comet is far away from the Sun, in the outer regions of the solar system.

When a comet gets close enough to the Sun, solar energy begins to vaporize the dust and water within it. The vaporized particles stream away from the head of the comet, pushed by the solar wind. A hazy, glowing coma forms around the head. A long tail forms, always pointing away from the Sun. The tail grows longest when the comet is closest to the Sun. A comet does not streak across the sky. Instead, it changes position slowly each night against the background of more distant stars. A comet may be visible for a period of several weeks, while it passes by Earth. It is thought that some comets come from the **Oort cloud,** a huge sphere around the solar system. When a comet breaks free, it falls slowly toward the Sun.

Meteoroids

Scattered through all the empty space between the planets are countless chunks of rock and metal called **meteoroids.** Meteoroids can be tiny or many meters across. When a meteoroid hits Earth's atmosphere, friction slows it down and heats it up. Usually, the meteoroid burns up in the sky and leaves behind a bright streak called a **meteor,** or shooting star. If a meteoroid survives the trip and lands on the ground, it becomes a **meteorite.**

During a meteor shower, you may see many meteors at once. Meteor showers happen several times each year. They are the result of Earth moving across the path that a comet once took. The tiny meteoroids left behind by a comet result in a shower of meteors.

Asteroids

Chunks of rock bigger than meteoroids are called **asteroids.** The smallest are less than a kilometer across and irregularly shaped. The largest known asteroid is Ceres. Ceres is shaped like a sphere and is about 940 kilometers in diameter. Most asteroids orbit the Sun in the asteroid belt between Mars and Jupiter. Astronomers had long thought there should be a planet in the gap between Mars and Jupiter. They found the "planet" Ceres in 1801. But, when three more "planets" were discovered in the same region, astronomers soon realized their mistake. There are over 20,000 numbered asteroids.

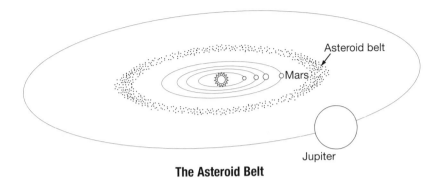

The Asteroid Belt

Some asteroids have more elliptical orbits. These orbits cause asteroids to veer out of the asteroid belt. Some of these asteroids cross the orbit of Earth. Will an asteroid collide with Earth some day? There is a chance it could happen. It is thought that the dinosaur extinction 65 million years ago was caused by an asteroid colliding with Earth.

■ PRACTICE 9: Comets, Meteoroids, and Asteroids

Decide if each statement that follows is true (**T**) or false (**F**). Write the correct letter on each line.

_____ **1.** During most of a comet's orbital period, the comet is far from the Sun.

_____ **2.** The Oort cloud is the glowing cloud around the head of a comet.

_____ **3.** When a meteorite falls to the ground, it is called a meteoroid.

_____ **4.** A meteor shower is a result of tiny meteoroids left behind by a comet.

_____ **5.** Most asteroids have orbits that cross Earth's orbit.

_____ **6.** The asteroid belt is between Mars and Jupiter.

LESSON 3: Earth's Moon

WORDS TO KNOW

apogee	new moon	tides
crescent moon	penumbra	totality
eclipse	perigee	umbra
full moon	phases	waning moon
gibbous moon	quarter moon	waxing moon
maria	satellite	
neap tides	spring tides	

About the Moon

As Earth orbits the Sun, it brings along a companion. That companion is the Moon, a natural **satellite** that orbits Earth. Have you ever wondered why the Moon orbits Earth instead of wandering through space? Or, why the planets follow their regular repeated orbits around the Sun? The reason is a combination of two basic laws of nature. The first law is that a moving object will continue moving in a straight line unless some outside force acts on it. Since the Moon and the planets are moving, they would move in a straight line forever until some outside force acted on them. There is no force of friction in space to slow them down. The only outside force is the force of gravity.

The second law is the law of gravity. This law states that every object in the universe attracts every other object.

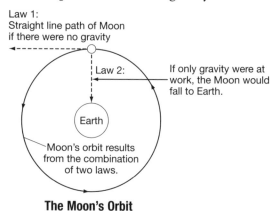

Law 1:
Straight line path of Moon
if there were no gravity

Law 2:

If only gravity were at work, the Moon would fall to Earth.

Earth

Moon's orbit results from the combination of two laws.

The Moon's Orbit

In space, the gravitational attraction between the Sun and the planets pulls the planets toward the Sun. The planets are constantly falling toward the Sun, but their forward motion keeps them circling around it instead. Earth's Moon stays in its orbit for the same reason. Earth and the Moon are close enough that their gravitational attraction overcomes the gravity of the Sun.

IN REAL LIFE

The laws of nature are at work right here on Earth. Seat belts are one way to prevent a moving object (you) from continuing to move forward (into the windshield) when the rest of the car is acted on by an outside force (a tree). Your body keeps moving 55 kilometers per hour, even though the car around you has come to a stop. The seat belt is the outside force that prevents you from slamming into the windshield at 55 kilometers per hour.

People first landed on the Moon in 1969 during the *Apollo 9* mission. During that and other *Apollo* missions, lunar rocks were collected and brought back to Earth. After analyzing the rocks, astronomers learned two things. First, the Moon is made of rocks very similar to those on Earth. Second, the rocks show that the Moon is 4.6 billion years old—the same age as Earth. Is the Moon just a huge chunk of rock that broke off when Earth was forming? Or, did the Moon form on its own, near Earth, at the same time that the rest of the solar system was forming? Astronomers still do not know exactly how the Moon was formed.

In either case, the Moon's earliest days as a satellite were spent being bombarded with rocks and debris. There is no atmosphere on the Moon. So, like Mercury, the impact craters are still there. Plus, new craters are made every time another meteorite falls to the surface of the Moon. The Moon's average distance from Earth is only 384,000 kilometers. The Moon's diameter is about 3400 kilometers. This means that the Moon is about 4 times smaller than Earth. Since the Moon is small, gravity is only $\frac{1}{6}$ as strong as it is on Earth. If you weigh 150 pounds on Earth, you would weigh only 25 pounds on the Moon.

The Moon does not shine on its own. Only the Sun, burning meteors, and glowing comets do that! What appears to be light from the Moon is actually reflected sunlight. Galileo looked at the Moon through his small telescope in 1610. He thought that the dark areas were filled with water. He named them **maria,** the Latin word for *seas*. However, there is no water on the Moon's surface.

The maria are actually smooth, dark plains of volcanic rock. Astronomers believe that there was a period when volcanoes were active on the Moon. During that time, lava filled in the basins of the largest impact craters. The lighter highlands are the areas that were not covered by lava. Today, there are no active volcanoes on the Moon.

■ PRACTICE 10: About the Moon

Decide if each statement that follows is true (**T**) or false (**F**). Write the correct letter on each line.

_____ **1.** The planets are constantly circling the Sun.

_____ **2.** The Moon orbits Earth because of a natural law that says all objects in space will move in circular paths.

_____ **3.** The Moon is the same age as Earth—4.6 billion years old.

_____ **4.** The Moon shines by reflected sunlight.

_____ **5.** Maria are dark areas of water on the Moon.

_____ **6.** There have never been volcanoes on the Moon.

_____ **7.** The highlands are lighter-colored areas that were not covered by lava.

Observing the Moon

Like the orbits of the other planets and moons in the solar system, the Moon's orbit is elliptical. The point in the Moon's orbit closest to Earth is called **perigee.** The farthest point is called **apogee.** Like the other planets and moons in the solar system, the Moon rotates, or spins, at the same time that it revolves. However, the Moon is unusual because it rotates and revolves at exactly the same rate. In the $29\frac{1}{2}$ days that it takes for the Moon to revolve around Earth, the Moon has rotated exactly once. The result is that the same side of the Moon always points in our direction. We cannot see the other side from Earth.

The Moon rises in the east and sets in the west each day because of Earth's rotation. Since the Moon is moving forward along its orbit, it rises about 50 minutes later each day. Each day, the Moon looks a little different from the way it did the day before. Its shape appears to change. The Moon's **phases** are the daily changes in the Moon's apparent shape. They result from the arrangement of the Sun, Earth, and Moon.

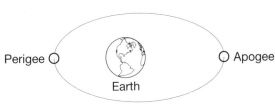

The Moon's Elliptical Orbit

At any given time, only one half of the Moon's surface is lit by the Sun. The other half is dark. The phase depends on how much of the lit-up side you can see. The Moon moves through its phases continually. While it is steadily growing larger in appearance, it is called a **waxing moon.** When it is growing smaller, it is called a **waning moon.**

New Moon

You cannot see a **new moon.** The entire lit-up side of the Moon faces away from Earth.

Crescent Moon

During a **crescent moon,** you see only a thin portion of the lit-up side. The rest of the lit-up side faces away from Earth. Crescent moons are visible mainly in the daytime. You may have seen the waxing crescent moon at twilight, following the setting Sun into the west.

Quarter Moon

During a **quarter moon,** you see exactly half of the lit-up side. A waxing quarter moon is also called a first quarter moon. It rises around noon and sets around midnight. A waning quarter moon, also called a last quarter moon, rises at midnight and sets around noon.

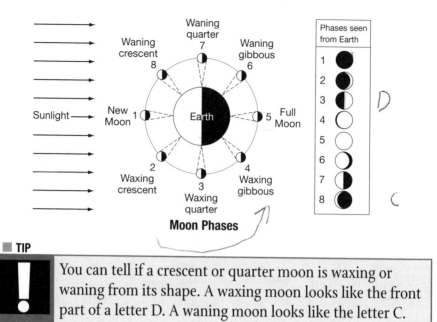

Moon Phases

TIP

You can tell if a crescent or quarter moon is waxing or waning from its shape. A waxing moon looks like the front part of a letter D. A waning moon looks like the letter C.

Gibbous Moon

During a **gibbous moon,** you see most of the Moon's lit-up side. A waxing gibbous moon rises in the mid-afternoon and sets in the early hours of the morning. A waning gibbous moon rises in the mid-evening and sets in the mid-morning.

Full Moon

During a **full moon,** you can see the entire lit-up face of the Moon. A full moon always rises at sunset and sets at sunrise. This is because the full moon and the Sun are in opposite parts of the sky.

■ PRACTICE 11: Observing the Moon

Decide if each statement that follows is true (**T**) or false (**F**). Write the correct letter on each line.

_____ **1.** The point in the Moon's orbit closest to Earth is called apogee.

_____ **2.** The side of the Moon facing in our direction is always the same.

_____ **3.** While the Moon is steadily growing larger, it is waxing.

_____ **4.** The full moon always rises at sunset.

_____ **5.** A waxing quarter moon is the same as a last quarter moon.

_____ **6.** The entire lit-up side of the Moon faces away from Earth during the full moon phase.

Eclipses

Solar Eclipse

An **eclipse** occurs when one object in space is shadowed by another. A solar eclipse happens when the Sun is blocked from view by the Moon. This can only happen during the new moon phase—when the Moon moves between the Sun and Earth. When you look at the Moon and Sun, they appear to be the same size. The Moon, smaller, yet closer to Earth,

The Moon and the Sun are different sizes, but they appear to be the same size because they are different distances from Earth.

exactly covers the Sun's disk. This is shown in the diagram.

The shadow cast by the Moon—or any object—has two parts. These shadows are called the umbra and the penumbra. The **umbra** is the area of total shadow. It is shaped like a long, narrow cone. The **penumbra** is the area of partial shadow that surrounds the umbra. Locations on Earth that fall within the small area of the umbra will see a total solar eclipse. Locations on Earth within the larger area of the penumbra will see a partial solar eclipse. During a partial solar eclipse, the Sun is only partly covered.

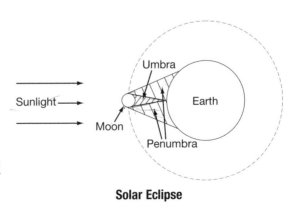

Solar Eclipse

At the start of a solar eclipse, the Moon moves along its orbit, covering more and more of the Sun. The sky does not noticeably darken until the Sun is mostly covered. At the moment of **totality,** when the Sun is completely blocked by the Moon, the sky is dark. Bright stars and planets become visible. It is at that one moment that the Sun's corona and chromosphere can be seen. The total solar eclipse ends as the Moon moves onward and the Sun is slowly uncovered.

TIP

Do not look directly at the Sun even during a total solar eclipse. The Sun's rays are still very dangerous, even if the Sun is covered by the Moon.

Lunar Eclipse

During a lunar eclipse, the Moon moves into the shadow cast by Earth. A lunar eclipse can happen only during the full moon phase, when Earth lies between the Sun and the Moon. Earth's shadow has a long cone-shaped umbra that extends far beyond the Moon. It is surrounded by a wide penumbra. A total lunar eclipse happens when the Moon is entirely within Earth's umbra. A partial lunar eclipse happens when the Moon is either partially in the umbra, or entirely in the penumbra.

You have a much better chance of seeing a lunar eclipse than a solar eclipse. All locations on Earth that have a clear view of the Moon will see the lunar eclipse when it happens. At the start of a lunar eclipse, the Moon first moves into Earth's penumbra, and then passes into the umbra. Because Earth's umbra is so large, totality lasts up to $1\frac{1}{2}$ hours. Finally, the Moon passes through the penumbra on the other side, and the eclipse is over.

During a total lunar eclipse, the Moon can still be seen. A small amount of sunlight passes through the rim of Earth's atmosphere and is bent toward the Moon. The light makes the eclipsed Moon look slightly reddish.

Why don't eclipses occur each month during the new and full moon phases? This does not happen because the Moon's orbit is not in exactly the same plane as Earth's orbit. The angle of the two orbits is about

5 degrees. Every so often, up to seven times per year, the Moon's orbit crosses Earth's orbit at the correct time for at least a partial eclipse to happen.

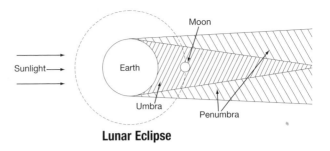

Sunlight→

Earth

Moon

Umbra

Penumbra

Lunar Eclipse

■ PRACTICE 12: Eclipses

Decide if each statement that follows is true (**T**) or false (**F**). Write the correct letter on each line.

_____ **1.** When the Sun is blocked by the Moon, it is a solar eclipse.

_____ **2.** For a solar eclipse, totality is when the Sun is completely blocked out by the Moon.

_____ **3.** The eclipsed Sun has a reddish look.

_____ **4.** Everybody who can see the Moon can see a lunar eclipse.

_____ **5.** A partial solar eclipse is visible from a larger area than a total solar eclipse.

Tides

The gravitational attraction between Earth and the Moon causes tides. Tides are the daily rise and fall of the ocean waters. The connection between the Moon and tides has been understood for many years. People noticed long ago that, like the Moon, the tides rise 50 minutes later each day. Tides result from the fact that the pull of gravity depends on the distance between two objects.

Look at the diagram on the right. The ocean water closest to the Moon (point A) is pulled toward the Moon more strongly than the solid Earth (point B). The ocean waters bulge outward toward the Moon, causing a direct high tide on that side of Earth. However, Earth

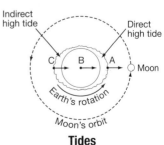

Indirect high tide

Direct high tide

C B A

Moon

Earth's rotation

Moon's orbit

Tides

is pulled more strongly toward the Moon than the ocean waters on the side of Earth farthest from the Moon (point C). These ocean waters also bulge outward, because Earth is pulled away from them. An indirect high tide takes place on the far side of Earth. The places in between have low tides.

Earth's rotation is what makes the ocean waters rise and fall on a regular basis at any one location. The time between peak high tide and low tide is a little over six hours.

The Sun's gravity also has an effect on tides. It can make the tides higher or lower than normal. During the new moon and full moon phases, the Sun lines up with Earth and the Moon. The Sun's gravity adds to the pull on the water. **Spring tides** are the especially high and especially low tides that occur at the new and full moon. During the quarter phases of the Moon, the Sun is not lined up with the Moon and Earth. Its gravity works against the Moon's gravity. **Neap tides** happen twice a month and are not as high or as low as normal.

IN REAL LIFE

If you live on the coast, you may have experienced flooding during astronomical high tides. These are spring tides that are higher than normal because the Moon is at perigee.

■ PRACTICE 13: Tides

Decide if each statement that follows is true (**T**) or false (**F**). Write the correct letter on each line.

_____ **1.** The tides rise 50 minutes later each day.

_____ **2.** A direct high tide takes place on the side of Earth farthest from the Moon.

_____ **3.** Tides result because the pull of gravity depends on the distance between two objects.

_____ **4.** At any one location, the daily high tides will alternate between spring tides and neap tides.

_____ **5.** Spring tides are especially high or especially low because the Sun lines up with the Moon and Earth.

LESSON 4: Observations from Spaceship Earth

GOAL: To understand day and night, the seasons, and constellations

WORDS TO KNOW

aphelion	equator	Polaris
asterisms	equinoxes	solstice
circumpolar	Northern Hemisphere	Southern Hemisphere
constellations	perihelion	

Observing Day and Night

From your observations of the cosmos, can you understand why ancient astronomers believed that Earth was the center of the universe? Like you, they saw the Sun and stars circle around Earth each day. To them, it appeared that Earth stood completely still in the center of a spinning universe.

Everyone knows that spaceship Earth is moving, but it does not feel like it. In 1530, Polish astronomer Nicolaus Copernicus was the first to suggest that it did. He made careful observations of the sky and concluded that the Sun was the center of the solar system. He believed that Earth, along with the planets, moved in orbits around the Sun. At the time, his theory was so controversial that it was called "false" and "absurd."

Of course, Copernicus was correct. The Sun is the center of the solar system. Earth orbits the Sun at an average distance of

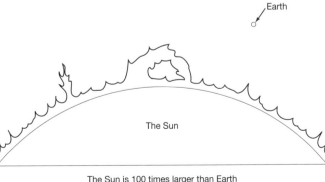

Earth

The Sun

The Sun is 100 times larger than Earth and 150 million kilometers away.

150 million kilometers. This distance is also called an astronomical unit or an AU. Earth is 1 AU from the Sun. With a diameter of about 12,700 kilometers, Earth is about 100 times smaller than the Sun. Spaceship Earth seems very small indeed when placed 150 million kilometers away.

TIP

To get a feel for the size and space in the solar system, imagine that Earth is a golf ball. The Sun would be a sphere about 4 meters in diameter—large enough to fit around a midsize car. How far apart are the Sun and Earth? On this scale, the golf ball used to model Earth would be $\frac{2}{5}$ of a kilometer from the Sun.

The rising and setting of the Sun, stars, and planets is due to Earth's rotation. Earth rotates around an imaginary axis that runs through the North and South poles. It rotates once every 24 hours, or once a day. The side of Earth facing the Sun experiences daytime. The other side experiences nighttime. Earth moves around the Sun in an elliptical orbit once a year. Its orbital period is $365\frac{1}{4}$ days. Every four years, there is a leap year to make up for the four extra quarter-days. Earth is closest to the Sun on January 2 when Earth is at **perihelion.** Earth is farthest from the Sun on July 4 when Earth is at **aphelion.**

Length of Day

At any one time, half of Earth is lit up by sunlight. The other half is dark, experiencing nighttime. If Earth's axis were straight up and down compared to its orbit, the length of day and night would be the same everywhere on Earth. Both would last for 12 hours. However, Earth's axis is tilted compared to the plane of Earth's orbit. As you can see in the diagram on the next page, the northern half of Earth, called the **Northern Hemisphere,** tilts toward the Sun on June 21. As Earth rotates on its axis, locations in the Northern Hemisphere are in sunlight more than they are in darkness. The result is the long summer days and short summer nights that are familiar to you. The length of day and night changes throughout the year, as Earth moves in its orbit.

While the Northern Hemisphere points toward the Sun, the southern half of the world, called the **Southern Hemisphere,** points away from the Sun. When the Northern Hemisphere experiences summer, the Southern Hemisphere experiences winter and short days. Its seasons are opposite those of the Northern Hemisphere. The two hemispheres are divided by the **equator,** which circles Earth halfway between the North and South Poles. If you were on the equator, you would be at the only location where days and nights are always 12 hours each, no matter what time of year.

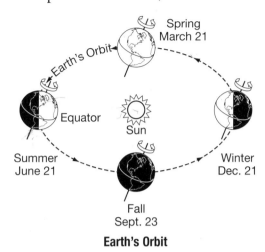

Earth's Orbit

■ PRACTICE 14: Observing Day and Night

Decide if each statement that follows is true (**T**) or false (**F**). Write the correct letter on each line.

_____ **1.** Nicolaus Copernicus believed that Earth does not move.

_____ **2.** The Sun is 100 times larger than Earth.

_____ **3.** Earth rotates on its axis twice a day.

_____ **4.** Earth is closest to the Sun on July 4.

_____ **5.** Earth's axis is tilted compared to the plane of its orbit.

_____ **6.** In the summer, days are longer than nights at the equator.

Observing the Seasons

It is not Earth's distance from the Sun that causes the seasons. After all, Earth is closest to the Sun when the Northern Hemisphere is having winter! The seasons are caused by the tilt of Earth's axis. From the North Pole, the axis points to a distant star called the North Star, or **Polaris.**

The first day of summer is called the summer **solstice.** In the Northern Hemisphere, the summer solstice is June 21. On that day, the Northern Hemisphere is pointed directly toward the Sun. There are more hours of daylight in the Northern Hemisphere on June 21 than any other day of the year. You have probably noticed that the Sun rises higher in the sky in the summer. When the Sun is high in the sky, Earth's rounded surface can soak up more of its energy. The Sun will rise to its highest point at noon on the summer solstice. On that day at the Tropic of Cancer, the Sun is directly overhead at noon.

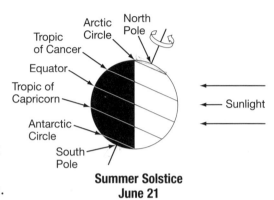

**Summer Solstice
June 21**

For places above the Arctic Circle, the Sun never sets on June 21. While the Northern Hemisphere experiences summer, the Southern Hemisphere experiences winter. Places below the Antarctic Circle have 24 hours of cold and darkness each day. As summer fades to winter in the north, winter gives way to summer in the south.

Winter begins on the winter solstice. In the Northern Hemisphere, the winter solstice is December 21. On that day, the Northern Hemisphere is pointed away from the Sun. At the North Pole, the Sun does not rise and will not be seen again for several months. December 21 is the shortest day of the year in the

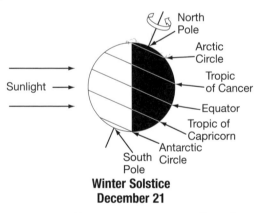

**Winter Solstice
December 21**

Northern Hemisphere. The Southern Hemisphere experiences its first day of summer on December 21. Below the equator, at the Tropic of Capricorn, the Sun is directly overhead.

As Earth moves along its orbit, it passes through two points where it does not tilt. The axis neither points toward nor away from the Sun. On these two days, called the **equinoxes,** all locations on Earth have 12 hours of daylight and 12 hours of nighttime. The spring equinox falls on March

21, the first day of spring. The fall equinox is on September 23, the first day of fall. At noon on the equinoxes, the Sun is directly overhead at the equator.

THINK ABOUT IT

Why would places north of the Arctic Circle be called the *land of the midnight sun*? Write your answer on a separate sheet of paper.

■ PRACTICE 15: Observing the Seasons

Circle the answer that correctly completes each of the following statements.

1. In the Northern Hemisphere, December 21 is the _____.
   a. summer solstice
   b. winter solstice
   c. fall equinox

2. For places above the Arctic Circle, the Sun never sets on the _____.
   a. summer solstice
   b. winter solstice
   c. equinoxes

3. At noon on June 21, the Sun is directly overhead at the _____.
   a. equator
   b. Tropic of Cancer
   c. Tropic of Capricorn

4. At noon on September 23, the Sun is directly overhead at the _____.
   a. equator
   b. Tropic of Cancer
   c. Tropic of Capricorn

5. The first day of spring is _____.
   a. March 21
   b. the spring equinox
   c. both *a* and *b*

Looking Outward at the Constellations

When you look outward from planet Earth, you can see a sky filled with thousands of stars. The sky looks about the same to you as it did to sky watchers of the past. To help make sense of the sky, they defined patterns among the stars they saw. These patterns are called **constellations.** Stars in a constellation only appear to be close to one another. In reality, the stars are separated by great distances.

There are 88 constellations in the sky. A little more than half of those are visible in the Northern Hemisphere at some point during the year. Sometimes, for convenience, people break up a big constellation into smaller star patterns, or group several constellations into one larger pattern. These patterns are called **asterisms.**

One important asterism is the Big Dipper, which is part of the constellation Ursa Major, the Great Bear. The two stars on the end of the bowl are called pointer stars. If you follow them across the sky, they point to Polaris, the North Star. Polaris is part of another asterism called the Little Dipper, which is part of a larger constellation called Ursa Minor, the Little Bear.

Polaris got its name because it happens to be directly overhead at the North Pole. If you were at the North Pole and paying close attention, you would notice that the background of stars slowly rotates around Polaris. While all the other stars appear to circle around it, Polaris stays in the same spot in the sky. In the United States, Polaris is not overhead. It appears lower in the northern sky the farther south you are. But from any one location, the position of Polaris remains fixed.

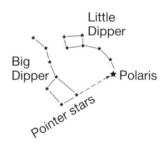

Constellations that circle Polaris, but never set below the horizon, are called **circumpolar** constellations. For most of the United States, Ursa Major and Ursa Minor are circumpolar. They

can be low or high in the sky, but they are always above the horizon. They never rise or set and can be seen any time of year.

In the winter, the night side of Earth looks out on a different part of the universe than in the summer. As a result, you will see different constellations in the summer and winter. The most famous winter constellation is Orion, the hunter. Like the names of all the constellations, Orion's name comes from Greek mythology. The brightest stars in Orion are Betelgeuse—a red supergiant, and Rigel—a blue supergiant. The best way to spot Orion is to look for the belt—three bright stars in a straight row.

The first stars to come out on a summer evening are three bright stars that make up the Summer Triangle. The Summer Triangle is not really a constellation. Each of the three stars belongs to a different constellation. The brightest star of the three is Vega, which is part of the constellation Lyra. Altair belongs to the constellation Aquila. Deneb is part of the constellation Cygnus.

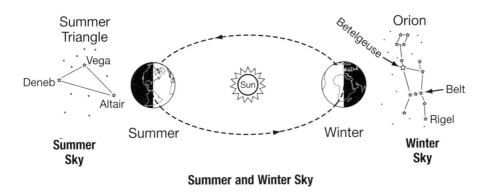

Summer and Winter Sky

If you, like ancient and modern astronomers, made careful observations of the sky at night, you would begin to notice "stars" that seem to wander over the background of fixed stars. These stars are actually the planets. The word *planet* means "wanderer." The wanderings of Venus and Mercury keep them close to the Sun. Mars, Jupiter, Saturn, and—on a clear night—Uranus, wander over a larger section of the sky. Their position in the night sky will depend on where they are in their orbit and where our own wandering "spaceship" is in its orbit.

■ PRACTICE 16: Looking Outward at the Constellations

Decide if each statement that follows is true (**T**) or false (**F**). Write the correct letter on each line.

_____ **1.** Stars in a constellation are really close together.

_____ **2.** Polaris can be found by the two pointer stars in the Big Dipper.

_____ **3.** Polaris will appear higher in the northern sky the farther south you go.

_____ **4.** For most of the United States, Orion is a circumpolar constellation.

_____ **5.** You see different constellations in the summer and winter.

_____ **6.** Orion is a winter constellation in the Northern Hemisphere.

_____ **7.** One of the first stars to come out on a summer evening is Betelgeuse.

_____ **8.** The planets wander against the background of stars.

UNIT 1 REVIEW

Circle the answer that correctly completes each of the following statements.

1. On the electromagnetic spectrum, the difference between light waves and radio waves is _____.
   a. only light waves are visible to us
   b. only radio waves carry energy
   c. only light waves travel at the speed of light

2. A star starts to glow when _____.
   a. it explodes into a supernova
   b. nuclear fusion begins in the core
   c. gravity pulls clouds of hydrogen gas within a galaxy

3. Compared to a smaller star, a large, massive star will burn _____.
   a. at the same rate
   b. much longer
   c. much more quickly

4. Supernovas are _____.
   a. explosions of large stars
   b. the cores of neutron stars
   c. black holes

5. Because of its impact craters, the Moon is most like planet _____.
   a. Earth
   b. Mercury
   c. Uranus

6. The _____ shines on its own.
   a. Moon
   b. Sun
   c. both *a* and *b*

7. The Jovian planets are made of mostly _____.
   a. rock
   b. metal
   c. gas

8. The best explanation for why the Moon causes tides is that _____.
   a. the Moon's gravity pulls harder on water than on land
   b. the Moon's gravity pulls most strongly on objects closest to it
   c. the Moon's gravity is always weaker than the Sun's gravity

9. Copernicus believed that _____.
   a. the Sun is the center of the universe
   b. the Sun is the center of the solar system
   c. Earth stands completely still in a spinning universe

10. In the Northern Hemisphere, summer begins on _____.
   a. July 4, at aphelion
   b. June 21, on the summer solstice
   c. March 21, on the spring equinox

UNIT 1 APPLICATION ACTIVITY 1
Gravitational Force and Planetary Orbit

You can demonstrate the effect of gravitational force on planetary orbit using common household materials.

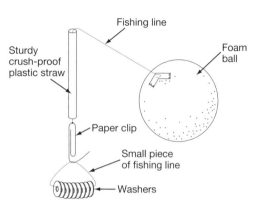

Thread a 50-cm length of nylon fishing line through a sturdy plastic straw (the crush-proof type). Tape a foam ball securely to one end of the line. Tie a paper clip to the other end of the line. Bend the end of the paper clip slightly to use as a hanger.

Cut a short piece of fishing line (about 5 cm long). Loop the line through five washers, and tie it securely. Hang the loop on the paper clip.

Work with a partner. With your hands in front of your body (approximately waist high), and using the straw as a handle, carefully whirl the ball around in a circle until the paper clip moves up to *just below* the bottom of the straw. Once this occurs, have your partner measure the amount of time it takes for the ball to complete 10 revolutions around the straw. Then, find the time needed for one revolution by dividing this time by 10.

_____ seconds ÷ 10 = _____ seconds = period of revolution

Record your data in the chart at the right.

No. of Washers	Period of Revolution
5	
10	
15	
20	
25	

Repeat steps 2 and 3, using 10, 15, 20, and 25 washers. Record each period of revolution in the chart.

1. What does the foam ball represent?

   _____

   _____

2. What is represented by the number of washers?

   _____

   _____

3. As the gravitational force increases, what happens to the period of revolution?

   _____

   _____

   _____

On a separate sheet of paper, draw a graph that illustrates the relationship between the gravitational force and the period of rotation.

4. How does this exercise relate to planetary motion?

   _____

   _____

   _____

   _____

   _____

UNIT 1 APPLICATION ACTIVITY 2

Relating Distance and Apparent Motion

Cut a sheet of $8\frac{1}{2}$-by-11-inch paper in half, lengthwise. Tape the two halves together, end to end, to make one long strip. Tape the strip along the baseboard of a wall. The paper represents distant space. Mark a point on the right side of the paper. Label this point "starting point."

Cut out four circles from another sheet of paper. Each circle should be about 5 cm in diameter. Label the circles Planet A, Planet B, Planet C, and Earth. Moving in a straight line away from the starting point on the wall, measure and place your circles on the floor as follows: At 20 cm, place "Planet C" on the floor. At 40 cm, place "Planet B" on the floor. At 80 cm, place "Planet A" on the floor. At 100 cm, place Earth on the floor.

Facing the wall, move Planets A, B, and C exactly 10 cm to the left, parallel to the wall. This represents the actual motion of the planets. Leave Earth in its original position.

With a meterstick, mark the point on the paper taped to the wall where a straight line running from the center of Earth through the center of Planet A would meet the paper. Mark and label this point as Point A on the paper. Repeat this with Planet B and with Planet C, marking and labeling the appropriate points on the paper on the wall.

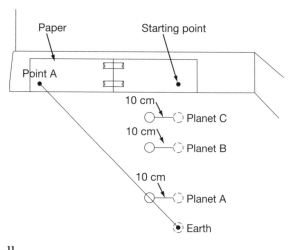

Measure the distances from the starting point to each of the new points marked on the paper. The distance between these points is called apparent distance, because, to an observer on Earth, the planets would have appeared to have moved that distance. Record these distances in the chart on the next page.

Planet	Actual Distance Moved	Apparent Distance Moved
A	10 cm	
B	10 cm	
C	10 cm	

1. Which planet appeared to move farthest? _____

2. Which planet appeared to move least? _____

3. How does apparent motion compare to actual motion in your model?

_____

_____

_____

_____

4. How does the distance of the observer from an object affect the apparent motion of the object, as seen by the observer?

_____

_____

_____

_____

_____

_____

_____

_____

UNIT 2

The Atmosphere Around Us

LESSON 5: The Atmosphere: Our Life Support System

 GOAL: To understand how Earth's atmosphere protects and supports life on Earth

WORDS TO KNOW

altitude	mesopause	stratosphere
contract	mesosphere	thermosphere
energy budget	ozone layer	tropopause
expands	scattered	troposphere
gas	sea level	uniform gases
greenhouse effect	solar energy	vacuum
ionosphere	solid	variable gases
liquid	stratopause	volcanic outgassing

The Origins of the Atmosphere

You live on the only planet in the solar system known to support life. Earth is like an oasis in the lifeless solar system. What makes Earth so different? Mainly, it is Earth's protective and supportive atmosphere. Earth's atmosphere is a thin layer of gas about 500 kilometers thick that surrounds the planet. Even though the atmosphere extends for miles above your head, it really is only a thin shell compared to the rest of Earth. This thin shell is the life support system aboard spaceship Earth.

The atmosphere gives Earth the oxygen you need to breathe. It filters out harmful radiation, traps heat, and cycles freshwater in the form of rain. Winds in the atmosphere circulate warmth and moisture around the entire planet.

When Earth formed 4.6 billion years ago, the thin gases that surrounded the planet soon escaped. For millions of years, there was no atmosphere on Earth. Between 3.5 and 4 billion years ago, gases trapped inside Earth were released during volcanic eruptions. This process is called **volcanic outgassing.** Volcanic outgassing produced a mixture of carbon dioxide, nitrogen, hydrogen, and water vapor.

In the early stages, Earth's atmosphere had no oxygen. Oxygen did not become part of the atmosphere until the first forms of life appeared about 3.5 billion years ago. These early life-forms were a type of bacteria that produced oxygen as a waste product. Over the next few billion years, oxygen gas built up in the atmosphere. Other life-forms evolved, and the amount of oxygen eventually leveled off about 400 million years ago.

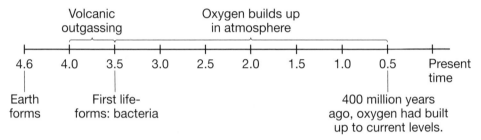

Time Line of Earth's Atmosphere
(in billions of years)

Today's atmosphere is made up of air (a mixture of invisible gases). Air is made up of 78% nitrogen, 21% oxygen, less than 1% argon, and trace (very small) amounts of neon, helium, methane, krypton, and hydrogen. These gases appear in the same percentages throughout most of the atmosphere. That is why they are called **uniform gases.**

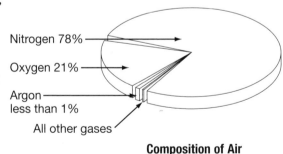

Composition of Air

Air also contains several variable gases. **Variable gases** are gases whose levels change depending on the location and weather at the time. Variable gases, such as ozone, water vapor, and carbon dioxide, make up a tiny percentage of the atmosphere. Yet, as you will see, they are critical to weather, climate, and life on Earth.

■ PRACTICE 17: The Origins of the Atmosphere

Circle the answer that correctly completes each of the following statements.

1. The atmosphere on Earth formed _____.
   a. when Earth formed
   b. through volcanic outgassing
   c. when the first forms of life appeared

2. Oxygen became part of the atmosphere about _____.
   a. 3.5 billion years ago
   b. 400 million years ago
   c. 4.6 billion years ago

3. The largest part of the atmosphere is _____.
   a. water vapor
   b. oxygen
   c. nitrogen

4. Gases whose levels change in the atmosphere are called _____.
   a. uniform gases
   b. variable gases
   c. volcanic gases

A Protective Atmosphere

The atmosphere contains four thin shells, or layers. The names given to the layers, from the inside out, are the troposphere, the stratosphere, the mesosphere, and the thermosphere. The height, or **altitude,** of each layer is measured from sea level. **Sea level** is the lowest part of the atmosphere. Sea level is the point midway between the highest seas and the lowest seas. The layers of the atmosphere are separated based on how temperature changes with altitude within each layer.

▦ THINK ABOUT IT

All of the following words end with the suffix –*sphere*: Atmo*sphere*, tropo*sphere*, strato*sphere*, meso*sphere*, thermo*sphere*. Can you explain why? Write your answer on a separate sheet of paper.

The tops of each of the lower three layers are called the **tropopause, stratopause,** and **mesopause.** These locations are the boundaries between each layer. At these boundaries, temperatures begin reversing direction. Temperatures *pause,* or stop increasing (or decreasing), with altitude and begin decreasing (or increasing) with altitude.

The Troposphere

You live in the troposphere. The **troposphere** is the bottom layer of the atmosphere. Temperatures in the troposphere decrease with altitude. Temperatures vary from 15°C at Earth's surface (sea level) to –55°C at the tropopause. On average, the troposphere extends to about 11 kilometers above sea level. It extends higher over the warm equator and lower over the poles. Only in the troposphere is the air "thick" enough to sustain most animal life. Also, most water vapor stays in the troposphere, along with all of Earth's weather systems.

The Stratosphere

The **stratosphere** lies above the troposphere and extends to an altitude of about 48 kilometers above sea level. Strong, steady winds blow through the stratosphere. In the stratosphere, air temperatures increase with altitude. The temperatures vary between –55°C at the beginning of the stratosphere to –3°C at the stratopause.

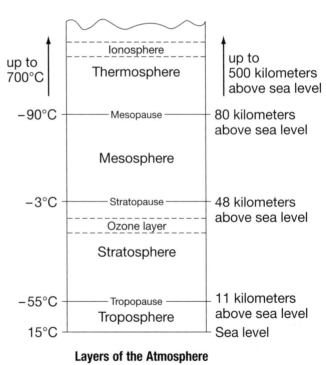

Layers of the Atmosphere

This increase in temperature occurs partly because of the energy absorbed by the ozone layer. The **ozone layer** is a protective layer of the variable gas called ozone. You and many other forms of life could not survive the intensity of the Sun's energy without the ozone layer. Ozone absorbs the Sun's harmful ultraviolet waves that can cause sunburn, skin cancer, and damage to crops.

Scientists are concerned about a thinning of the ozone layer in locations over Antarctica and the Arctic. This thinning, also called the ozone hole, constantly changes. Measurements have shown that each year the hole gets a little larger. The ozone hole is caused by pollutants called chlorofluorocarbons, or CFCs, which are widely used as coolants in refrigerators and air conditioners. Life on Earth depends on the protection offered by the ozone layer. Countries all over the world have agreed to reduce the use of CFCs.

The Mesosphere

The **mesosphere** lies between 48 and 80 kilometers above sea level. In the mesosphere, temperatures decrease with altitude. At the mesopause, air temperatures drop to $-90°C$, which is the lowest temperature in the entire atmosphere.

The Thermosphere

The **thermosphere** begins at an altitude of 80 kilometers and extends to about 500 kilometers above sea level. Here, the air is no longer the same mixture of uniform gases as in the lower atmosphere. Instead, the gas particles are so spread out that each gas settles into its own layer. The particles of gas within the thermosphere absorb solar energy. The result is that temperatures rise within the thermosphere to about 700°C. Most meteors burn up on their way through the thermosphere.

Within the thermosphere, there is a layer called the **ionosphere.** The atmospheric gases of the ionosphere are ionized, or electrically charged. This allows the ionosphere to reflect short-wavelength radio waves, making long distance radio communication possible.

■ PRACTICE 18: A Protective Atmosphere

Look at the list of words below. Fill in each line with the letter of the correct word. (*Hint:* There may be more than one answer for each line.)

_____ 1. contains the ozone layer

_____ 2. has the lowest temperature in the atmosphere

_____ 3. reflects radio waves

_____ 4. location of water vapor and weather

_____ 5. contains the ionosphere

_____ 6. where temperature decreases with altitude

_____ 7. where temperature increases with altitude

_____ 8. absorbs energy

_____ 9. boundaries between layers

_____ 10. does not have uniform gases

a. troposphere

b. stratosphere

c. mesosphere

d. thermosphere

e. tropopause

f. mesopause

g. stratopause

h. ionosphere

i. ozone layer

A Warm Atmosphere

Planet Earth, over 149 million kilometers from the Sun, collects only a tiny fraction of the Sun's energy. That tiny fraction of energy is the engine that drives Earth's weather systems. It also keeps the planet warm enough for life. The Sun's energy, called **solar energy,** reaches the outer part of Earth's atmosphere after passing through the vacuum of space. Of all the solar energy that reaches the outer layers of Earth's atmosphere, only about half of it ever reaches Earth's surface. What happens to the rest of it? The answer can be found by looking at Earth's energy budget. The **energy budget** is an accounting of how Earth uses the incoming solar energy.

Once the Sun's energy enters the atmosphere, it can be either absorbed, reflected, or scattered. Some energy is absorbed by the ozone layer, water vapor, and dust. Clouds both reflect and absorb solar energy. Some of the energy is **scattered,** or spread out in all directions, by particles of air. Only 55% of the Sun's energy actually makes it through the atmosphere to Earth's surface. (To see exactly where the solar energy goes, refer to the figure on the right.) But not all of that energy goes into heating Earth. About 4% of the Sun's energy is reflected right back out into space by Earth's surface.

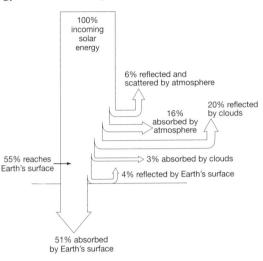

Earth's Energy Budget

The remaining 51% of the Sun's energy goes into heating Earth's surface (the ground). This energy is delivered to Earth in the form of light. Once the energy is absorbed by the ground, it turns around and becomes the source of heat for the atmosphere. Thus, the atmosphere is not heated directly by the Sun's energy. Instead, the atmosphere is heated by the ground. This explains why the warmest air is in the bottom of the troposphere.

The ground absorbs the light and returns the energy to the air in the form of heat. When the heat eventually escapes from Earth's atmosphere, the energy budget is a balanced budget. The energy may come in one form and leave in another, but all the Sun's energy has been accounted for.

IN REAL LIFE

Why is the sky blue? It has to do with how particles in the atmosphere scatter light in all directions. Blue light is scattered more than other colors, making the sky look blue.

The Greenhouse Effect

The atmosphere is heated by the ground because gases in the air absorb the heat. Carbon dioxide and water vapor, two variable gases, are called greenhouse gases. Greenhouse gases in the atmosphere act like the glass walls of a greenhouse. Light energy can easily pass through, but some of the heat energy is trapped.

The **greenhouse effect** refers to the way certain gases in the air trap heat. The greenhouse effect provides Earth with a warm blanket of air. The blanket keeps us warm both day and night. Without an atmosphere to keep us warm, air temperatures would drop to −140°C.

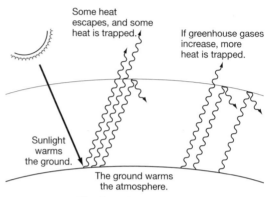

The Greenhouse Effect

You may have heard news stories about the greenhouse effect. Many scientists are concerned that it is getting stronger. Their fear is based on the increasing levels of carbon dioxide and water vapor in the atmosphere. Is Earth really getting hotter? That is the topic of much debate. You will learn more in Lesson 8, page 96, about the greenhouse effect and climate change.

■ PRACTICE 19: A Warm Atmosphere

Decide if each statement that follows is true (**T**) or false (**F**). Write the correct letter on each line.

_____ **1.** The Sun is an important driving force behind Earth's weather systems.

_____ **2.** The ground reflects 51% of the incoming solar energy.

_____ **3.** The atmosphere is heated directly by the Sun's energy.

_____ **4.** Carbon dioxide levels are increasing.

_____ **5.** Water vapor is a greenhouse gas.

An Atmosphere of Gas

What is gas? Gas is a form of matter. All matter can be thought of as a collection of tiny particles. There are three forms of matter: solid, liquid, and gas. The particles are arranged differently in each form. In a **solid,** the particles are packed closely together and cannot move about. As a result, solids are hard and keep their shape. In a **liquid,** particles are not arranged in any particular way. They move around freely and constantly, but always stay in close contact with one another. A liquid can change its shape so that it will take on the shape of its container.

Solid

Liquid

In a **gas** such as air, particles move about very quickly and do not stay in contact with one another. There is much more space between the particles in a gas than there is between the particles in a liquid or a solid. Since you cannot see air, how do you know it is there? You feel air when the particles all move together in the same direction. That is what happens when the wind blows.

Gas

Earth's atmosphere is a mixture of invisible particles of air. The air particles are pulled toward Earth by gravity. Gravity keeps our atmosphere from drifting away. Particles above push down on the lower particles. As a result, air particles are closer together in the troposphere than they are in the upper layers of the atmosphere. Half of the air particles in the atmosphere are in the bottom 5.6 kilometers of the troposphere. Moving away from Earth, the number of air particles thins out rapidly. There is no exact boundary to Earth's atmosphere. Gas particles become fewer and farther between at higher altitudes. Eventually, there is just a vacuum. A **vacuum** is space that has few particles of matter.

How Air Heats Up

When air is heated by the ground, the particles move about more quickly. In doing so, they move farther away from one another. The same number of particles takes up more space. The result is that the warm air **expands,** or gets larger, and rises. This is because it is less dense than the air near it.

When the air cools, the particles move more slowly and **contract,** or come closer together. Cooled air sinks toward the ground, is heated again, and rises.

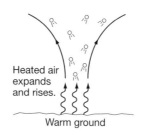

Heated air expands and rises.

Warm ground

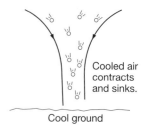

Cooled air contracts and sinks.

Cool ground

IN REAL LIFE

Have you ever heard somebody say "heat rises"? The next time someone says that, you can correct him or her. It is not *heat* that rises, but *heated air.* Heated air rises because it is less dense than the air around it. Hot-air balloonists take advantage of this fact by heating the air in the balloon to make it rise and allowing the air to cool so the balloon will come back down.

■ PRACTICE 20: An Atmosphere of Gas

Circle the answer that correctly completes each of the following statements.

1. The form of matter in which particles cannot move about is _____.
   a. gas
   b. solid
   c. liquid

2. The particles of air are held to Earth by _____.
   a. the atmosphere
   b. a vacuum
   c. gravity

3. When air heats up, the particles _____.
   a. move more quickly
   b. move closer to one another
   c. do not move

4. It is true that _____.
   a. warm air rises
   b. cool air rises
   c. heat rises

LESSON 6: Weather in the Atmosphere

GOAL: To understand the tools that meteorologists use to predict weather

WORDS TO KNOW

air pressure	fog	specific humidity
barometer	frost	stratus
cirrus	humidity	temperature
condensation	isobars	temperature inversion
cumulonimbus	millibars	thermometer
cumulus	nimbostratus	water cycle
dew	precipitation	weather
dew point	relative humidity	wind chill factor
evaporation	saturated	

Temperature and Air Pressure

What is the weather outside today? Is it cold and windy? Is it raining? Are the skies clear? **Weather** is the day-to-day change that takes place in the troposphere. Weather is caused by the interaction of the Sun, land, water, and air. The study of Earth's weather is the work of meteorologists. Meteorologists pay close attention to air pressure, temperature, and humidity.

Temperature

For most of us, temperature is the only weather information we need. If we know the temperature, we know how to dress for the day. To the meteorologist, temperature is just one tool used to predict the weather. **Temperature** is a measure of the heat of air particles. Heat tells us how much energy exists in the particles. Higher heat means greater energy.

Air particles move around in different directions all the time. The hotter the air, the faster the air particles move. The faster the air particles move, the more energy they carry with them.

A **thermometer** is an instrument used to measure temperature. The liquid in a thermometer is alcohol (with a red color). When alcohol absorbs heat from the air, it expands and moves up the tube. Thermometers measure temperature in degrees. There are two commonly used temperature scales, the Fahrenheit scale (°F) and the Celsius scale (°C). On the Fahrenheit scale, water freezes at 32°F and boils at 212°F. On the Celsius scale, water freezes at 0°C and boils at 100°C.

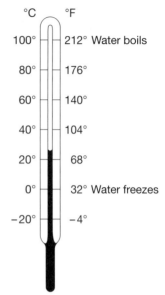

Wind Chill Factor

Sometimes how cold you feel has very little to do with air temperature. If the wind is blowing, you feel colder, even though the air temperature has not changed. The **wind chill factor** tells you what temperature the air actually *feels* like. When air is not moving, your body heats a thin layer of air surrounding it. The air is like a blanket that lets you stay warm in the winter, but can make you too hot in the summer. When the wind blows, this thin layer is blown away. The faster the wind blows, the more heat is lost from your body. Summer winds are refreshing, but winter winds can be dangerous.

The table on the next page shows how meteorologists determine the wind chill factor. To use the table, find the wind speed in the first column. Then move across the column until you are under the correct air temperature. The number in the box is the wind chill factor. For example, if the wind speed is 40 kilometers per hour (km/h) and the air temperature is 0°C, the wind chill factor is –13°C, or 13°C below zero.

Wind Chill Equivalent Temperature

Wind Speed (km/h)	Temperature (Celsius)							
	0	–5	–10	–15	–20	–25	–30	–35
10	–2	–7	–12	–17	–22	–27	–32	–38
20	–7	–13	–19	–25	–31	–37	–43	–50
30	–11	–17	–24	–31	–37	–44	–50	–57
40	–13	–20	–27	–34	–41	–48	–55	–62
50	–15	–22	–29	–36	–44	–51	–58	–66
60	–16	–23	–31	–38	–45	–53	–60	–68

THINK ABOUT IT

Use the table above to find the wind chill factor when the air temperature is –5°C and the wind speed is 10 km/h. Can you make an estimate of the wind chill factor at –5°C if the wind is 15 km/h? Write your answer on a separate sheet of paper.

Air Pressure

Although the atmosphere is invisible, it weighs over 5,000,000 trillion kilograms! If you were at sea level, the weight of the air pressing down on you would be 1.03 kilograms per square centimeter. The weight of air on a given area is called **air pressure.** Air pressure pushes equally in all directions. The pressure on the top of your head is the same as the pressure on the sides of your body. This is because the air particles are moving in all directions, pushing equally hard.

Meteorologists use barometers to measure air pressure. A **barometer** is an instrument that responds to the amount of air pressing down on it. In a mercury barometer, the level of mercury in a tube will rise and fall with changing air pressure. The level is measured in inches. Thus, meteorologists will often report air pressure in terms of *inches of mercury.* Pressure can also be expressed in **millibars,** a metric unit. A meteorologist expresses the air pressure at sea level as 1013.25 millibars.

Air pressure drops with altitude because there are fewer air particles higher in the atmosphere. Have you ever climbed a mountain? Air pressure at the top of a mountain is lower than air pressure at sea level. Mountain climbers know that it takes time to adjust to the thinner air at high altitudes. However, meteorologists are interested in how air pressure changes because of weather conditions, not because of altitude. For that reason, all air pressure readings are adjusted to indicate what the air pressure would be at sea level.

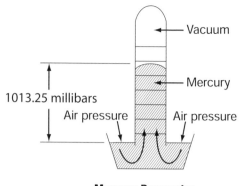

Mercury Barometer

Air pressure in an area will change on a daily basis. Warm air is less dense and, in general, has a lower air pressure than cooler air. The National Weather

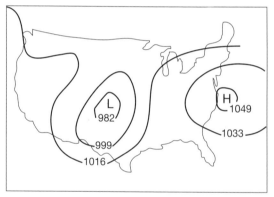

Isobars on a Weather Map

Service prints a weather map such as the one above each day. The weather map includes pressure readings taken at the same time all around the country. The pressure readings can be used to produce a map of isobars. **Isobars** are closed curves that join points of equal air pressure on a weather map.

The centers of the rings of the isobars are either low-pressure centers, where air pressure is lowest, or high-pressure centers, where air pressure is highest. The surrounding areas are either low-pressure areas or high pressure areas. In general, low-pressure areas bring rainy weather, while high-pressure areas bring clear skies. By measuring air pressure each day and using weather maps, meteorologists can try to predict what the weather will be in your area tomorrow.

■ PRACTICE 21: Temperature and Air Pressure

Decide if each statement that follows is true (**T**) or false (**F**). Write the correct letter on each line.

_____ **1.** Thermometers work because the liquid inside expands when it gets hot.

_____ **2.** There is no difference between 0°C and 32°F.

_____ **3.** When the wind blows, the air temperature goes down.

_____ **4.** At –10°C and with winds at 40 km/h, the wind chill factor is –17°C.

_____ **5.** A barometer measures air pressure.

_____ **6.** Isobars are lines of equal temperature.

_____ **7.** The center of a low-pressure area has the lowest pressure.

Humidity

Humidity is the amount of moisture, or invisible water vapor, in the atmosphere. In the lower troposphere, air can contain anywhere from 0% to 4% water vapor. This tiny amount plays a major role in our daily weather. Water is unique in that it can be found in all forms in the atmosphere. It can be found as a solid (ice and snow), as a liquid (rain), and as a gas (water vapor). The way the atmosphere continually circulates and recycles Earth's water is known as the **water cycle.** River, lake, and ocean waters are all sources of water vapor. Water vapor is a source of clouds and rain. Rain is a source feeding the rivers, lakes, and oceans. Water vapor is also a heat-trapping greenhouse gas.

■ TIP

 Water in the form of gas is called water vapor. *Vapor* is the gas form of any matter that can exist as both a liquid and a gas at normal temperatures and pressure.

Like all matter, water can be thought of as a collection of particles. For water to change from a liquid to a gas, particles in liquid water must move quickly enough to break away from the other water particles. This process is called **evaporation.** Heating the water will help the process along. (Remember, heat makes particles in matter move faster.) When water boils, all the particles are moving fast enough to eventually escape from the water's surface.

Water does not have to be boiling to evaporate. It will evaporate at lower temperatures, though this will occur more slowly. Collisions among the moving particles propel some of them quickly enough to escape. Once water vapor particles enter the air, they replace an equal volume of air particles. Water vapor particles weigh less than an equal number of air particles. Thus, humid air is less dense and at a lower pressure than dry air. In general, when air pressure drops, it usually means that more humid air is moving in. When air pressure rises, it means drier air is on its way.

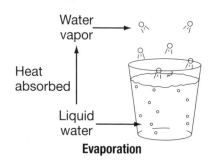

Evaporation

The atmosphere gains moisture through evaporation and loses it through condensation. **Condensation** is when water vapor changes from vapor to liquid water. Condensation occurs whenever water vapor particles slow down enough to return to a liquid form. In the atmosphere, condensation is the process that produces dew, frost, fog, clouds, and rain. However, there must be a surface onto which the water vapor can condense. Water vapor close to the ground will condense onto Earth's surface. Water vapor at higher levels will condense onto the numerous tiny bits of dust, salt, pollen, and pollution in the air.

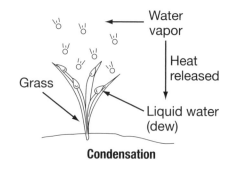

Condensation

When water evaporates, it absorbs some of the heat energy in the water. The heat is carried into the atmosphere by the water vapor. When the water vapor cools and condenses, it releases the heat energy. The heat released into the air plays an important role in the formation of clouds. You will learn more about the formation of clouds on page 73.

Relative Humidity

The exact amount of water vapor in the air is called the **specific humidity.** But meteorologists are more interested in the relative humidity. **Relative humidity** is the amount of water vapor the air holds compared to how much it can hold. Relative humidity compares specific humidity to the total possible humidity. If the relative humidity is 100%, the air is full, or **saturated.** If the relative humidity is 50%, the air is only half full of water vapor.

The relative humidity can change in two important ways. First, relative humidity will increase when specific humidity is increased. For example, a nearby ocean can be a source of water vapor and increase the specific humidity of air along the shore. Second, relative humidity will increase when temperature decreases. This happens because cold air cannot hold as much water vapor as warm air can. The same amount of water vapor will fill warm air to 50%, but colder air to 100%.

Suppose during a summer day that the relative humidity is 50%, as shown in the graph below. When night falls and the air cools, the amount of total possible humidity the air can hold decreases. The amount of water vapor, or the specific humidity, does not change. Eventually, the air will cool to its dew-point temperature, as shown in the middle graph. At the **dew point,** or the temperature at which water vapor condenses, relative humidity is 100% and the air is saturated. The specific humidity equals the total possible humidity in the air. Further cooling will force the water vapor out of the air, as shown in the graph on the right. The air stays saturated with a relative humidity of 100%. The water vapor condenses to form dew or fog.

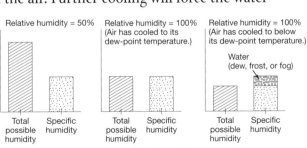

Relative Humidity

Dew, Frost, and Fog

Dew is water vapor that condenses onto a cold surface. When dew forms, only the air near the cold surface is cooled below the dew-point temperature. The cold surface can be the ground at night, an icy glass, or a cold windshield. Car defrosters control condensation by warming the windshield. Frost forms in the same way as dew. However, for frost to form, the cold surface must be below freezing (0°C). If a whole body of air is cooled below its dew-point temperature, fog will form. You may have seen fog form near a lake or an ocean when warm, humid air blows over colder water.

■ PRACTICE 22: Humidity

Look at the list of terms below. Fill in each line with the letter of the term that correctly completes each statement.

_____ 1. The way the atmosphere circulates water is known as the _____.

_____ 2. When the air is saturated the _____ is 100%.

_____ 3. The amount of moisture in the air is called _____.

_____ 4. When water vapor _____, it releases heat into the air.

_____ 5. When water _____, water vapor particles escape from the water's surface.

_____ 6. Fog forms when a whole body of air is cooled below its _____.

a. condenses

b. dew-point temperature

c. evaporates

d. humidity

e. relative humidity

f. water cycle

Clouds and Rain

A cloud is nothing more than fog in the sky. Clouds form in the same way that fog does—humid air is cooled below its dew-point temperature and condensation begins. Condensation produces tiny water droplets or ice crystals that form around the bits of dust, salt, pollen, or pollution in the air. Cloud droplets are so small that they easily stay aloft. Clouds can tell you what type of weather has just passed through. They can also tell you what type of weather you have now, and, more importantly, what type of weather to expect.

There are three different cloud types—cirrus, cumulus, and stratus. All other types are variations of these. If the cloud is a rain cloud, the term *nimbo-* or *-nimbus* (Latin for *rain*) is added to the cloud name. If a cloud forms at a higher-than-normal altitude, the term *alto-* (Latin for *high*) is added to it. The cloud types are shown in the illustration on page 74.

Cumulus clouds are fair-weather clouds that form low in the sky. They have flat bottoms and puffy, rounded tops. Cumulus clouds develop from warm air rising over heated land. When the warm air cools to its dew-point temperature, the moisture condenses and the cloud is born. The flat base of the cloud marks the dew-point level, or the altitude at which the air has cooled to its dew-point temperature.

As condensation continues in a cumulus cloud, heat is released from the water vapor. This makes the moist air in the cloud warmer than the drier air outside the cloud. Thus, the moist air keeps rising upward, producing the cloud's puffy, rounded top. Eventually, the cloud cools to the same temperature as the air outside it. That is when it stops growing. The term meteorologists use for the cooler air outside a cumulus cloud is unstable. If there is only a thin layer of unstable air, the cumulus clouds are small. If there is a deep layer of unstable air, powerful, billowing cumulonimbus clouds will form. **Cumulonimbus** clouds are the clouds of thunderstorms. Very tall cumulonimbus clouds have anvil-shaped tops blown by strong winds in the upper atmosphere. You will learn more about cumulonimbus clouds in Lesson 8 on page 90.

Stratus clouds are low, gray sheets that completely cover the sky. They form in stable air where the air is not rising. **Nimbostratus** clouds are thicker and darker than stratus clouds. These are the clouds that bring steady rain or snow.

Cirrus clouds are the highest of all clouds. At high altitudes, the air is very cold and has little water vapor. Thus, cirrus clouds are thin and feathery and made of ice crystals.

Stratocumulus clouds form large, gray rolls across the sky. Altocumulus clouds form higher in the sky than cumulus clouds. They look like puffy sheep. Cirrocumulus clouds are high, thin clouds that are grouped in such a way that they resemble the patterns on a mackerel's back, making what is referred to as a "mackerel sky." Altostratus clouds are bluish-gray sheets of clouds, thin enough for a weak sun to shine through. Cirrostratus clouds are high, thin sheets that sometimes cause rings around the Moon.

IN REAL LIFE

If you see cirrus clouds moving in from the west, it may mean wet weather is a few days away. If the cirrus clouds give way to high, thin sheets of cirrostratus clouds, you can be sure rain or snow is on the way.

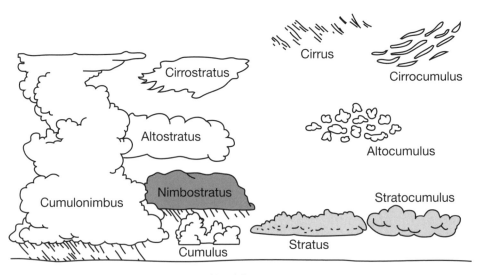

Cloud Types

Precipitation

Precipitation is water, in any form, falling from clouds. Precipitation can be rain, drizzle, freezing rain, snow, sleet, or hail. Precipitation begins only when the tiny droplets or ice crystals in a cloud grow heavy enough. Droplets within the cloud grow from collisions with other droplets. Ice crystals in the cloud will grow as more and more moisture condenses onto the crystal. When the droplets or ice crystals get heavy enough, they begin their fall toward the ground. Often, ice crystals will melt into rain while falling through warmer air.

THINK ABOUT IT

Sometimes water vapor in a cloud condenses around particles of sulfur dioxide or nitrogen oxide that result from the burning of fossil fuels. If this cloud produces rain, it will be a kind of rain you may have heard of. Do you know what it is? Write your answer on a separate sheet of paper.

Drizzle is fine, thin rain that falls slowly to the ground. Drizzle drops are about one-quarter the size of raindrops. They produce a gentle shower. The largest raindrops are only a few millimeters in diameter. Larger raindrops may form, but will usually break apart as they fall to the ground.

Snowflakes are beautiful, six-pointed crystals. When the air is very cold, snow reaches the ground as individual snowflakes. If the air is warm, the flakes may stick together to form large clumps. Sleet forms during a temperature inversion. **Temperature inversion** is when the air grows colder closer to the ground. Rain falling from a cloud freezes into pellets of ice, or sleet, before hitting the ground. Freezing rain occurs when rain falls and freezes instantly when it hits the frozen ground. Damaging ice storms are the result of freezing rain.

Hail forms in cumulonimbus clouds, where tremendous updrafts keep the hail from falling to the ground. Each time the hail begins to fall, another updraft

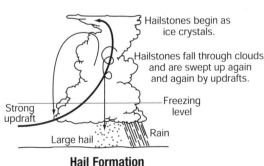

Hail Formation

carries it up through the cloud. A hailstone starts as an ice crystal and builds up in layers. Another layer of ice is added each time the hailstone passes through the cloud.

■ PRACTICE 23: Clouds and Rain

Circle the answer that correctly completes each of the following statements.

1. The dew-point level for a cumulus cloud is _____.
    a. the temperature inside the cloud
    b. the top of the cloud
    c. the base of the cloud

2. The term that is added to the name of a rain cloud is _____.
    a. *alto-*
    b. *nimbo-*
    c. *cirrus-*

3. Clouds that form in unstable air are _____.
    a. stratus
    b. cumulus
    c. both *a* and *b*

4. The highest clouds are _____.
    a. cirrus
    b. stratus
    c. cumulus

5. When there is a temperature inversion, there may be _____.
    a. freezing rain
    b. hail
    c. sleet

6. When a hailstone is carried up through a cloud, _____.
    a. the hailstone breaks apart
    b. another layer of ice is added
    c. another layer of ice is removed

LESSON 7: Winds in the Atmosphere

GOAL: To compare and contrast the winds that flow over Earth

WORDS TO KNOW

convection cell	monsoon winds	specific heat
Coriolis effect	planetary winds	trade winds
doldrums	pressure gradient	westerlies
jet streams	prevailing winds	

Wind

What makes the wind blow? All winds are the result of uneven heating. When one body of air is heated more than another, air pressure is uneven. Why? As heated air expands, the particles move farther apart. With fewer air particles, the same volume of air weighs less and air pressure drops. Air from nearby areas of higher pressure will rush toward the low-pressure area. Everywhere on Earth, air moves from areas of high pressure to areas of low pressure.

TIP

Think of a balloon filled with air. The air in the balloon is at a higher pressure than the air outside the balloon. Releasing the air in the balloon creates a "wind" of air moving from a high-pressure area to a low-pressure area.

The strength of the winds will depend on how quickly the air pressure changes between two locations. Large changes in air pressure over a short distance will produce strong winds. The rate at which air pressure changes is called the **pressure gradient.** Isobars on a weather map can be used to determine the pressure gradient. When isobars are close together, there is a larger pressure gradient, and the winds in the area are strong. When isobars are far apart, there is a smaller pressure gradient, and the winds are weak.

Winds develop as air moves from areas of high pressure toward areas of low pressure. However, the winds do not take a direct path. Instead, they curve away from the high-pressure area and spiral in toward the low-pressure area. This is a result of the Coriolis effect. The **Coriolis effect** is the change in the path of any object traveling above Earth's surface.

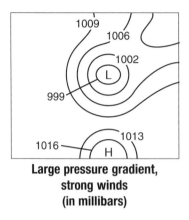

Large pressure gradient, strong winds (in millibars)

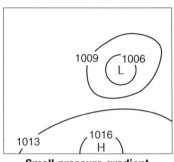

Small pressure gradient, weak winds (in millibars)

The Coriolis effect is caused by Earth's rotation. Imagine wind leaving the North Pole heading south toward the point labeled A in the diagram on the right. As Earth keeps rotating to the east, the wind seems to veer off toward point B in the west. The path of the wind is not straight. It is curved.

The Coriolis effect makes wind or any airborne object in the Northern Hemisphere veer off to the right. In the Southern Hemisphere, winds will veer off to the left. Thus, winds moving toward a low-pressure center will continually veer off their path. The result is that in the Northern Hemisphere, winds spiral in toward a low-pressure center in a counterclockwise direction. Winds spiral away from a high-pressure center in a clockwise direction. The Coriolis effect produces the opposite result in the Southern Hemisphere.

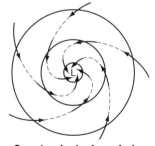

Counterclockwise winds in a low-pressure area

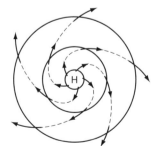

Clockwise winds in a high-pressure area

■ PRACTICE 24: Wind

Decide if each statement that follows is true **(T)** or false **(F)**. Write the correct letter on each line.

_____ **1.** Cool air moves from areas of high pressure to areas of low pressure.

_____ **2.** When isobars are close together, there is a small pressure gradient.

_____ **3.** Earth's rotation causes the Coriolis effect.

_____ **4.** The Coriolis effect causes winds to veer off to the right in the Northern Hemisphere.

_____ **5.** Winds spiral in toward a low-pressure system in a clockwise direction in the Northern Hemisphere.

Local Winds

Like winds in high-pressure and low-pressure areas, local winds arise from the uneven heating of Earth's surface. Local winds can blow in any direction, but only over an area of 80 kilometers or less. The Coriolis effect does not influence winds over such a small area. In any local area, winds can form because of the uneven heating of Earth's seashores and oceans or mountains and valleys.

Seashores and Oceans

If you live near a large body of water, you already know that the water keeps the air cool in the summer and warm in the winter. Water is slow to heat up and equally slow to cool off. This is another way of saying that water has a high specific heat. The **specific heat** of a material refers to the amount of energy needed to raise 1 gram of the material by 1 degree Celsius. Water needs to absorb a lot of energy to produce a temperature change. Place a glass of water and a rock of the same mass in the sun. The rock will get hot long before the water, even though they both receive the same amount of energy. Once the water gets hot, however, it will cool off more slowly than the rock.

Why does it take so long to boil water? Why does aluminum foil cool off more quickly than the food inside? Write your answer on a separate sheet of paper.

In the summer, the same amount of solar energy falls on a lake as on the sandy beach next to it. The temperature of the lake barely changes, while the sand can get hot enough to burn your feet. In the winter, the ground freezes before any ice forms on the lake. Earth's waters have a higher specific heat than sand, rock, dirt, asphalt, or any land material on Earth. Land warms up and cools down faster than oceans.

Remember that air is heated by the ground or the ocean beneath it. Therefore, ocean air stays cooler than inland air in the summer. In the winter, ocean air is warmer than inland air. A large body of water tends to keep nearby air temperatures moderate all year long.

Sea breezes and land breezes are examples of local winds that result from uneven heating. During the day, land near the coast is warmer than the water. The air over the land heats up and expands upward, creating a low-pressure area on a local level. The cool, higher pressure ocean air moves in to replace the rising warm air. The movement of ocean air toward the land is called a sea breeze. The rising inland air spreads out, cools, and sinks again over the ocean. The air circulates in a **convection cell,** as shown in the diagram on the right.

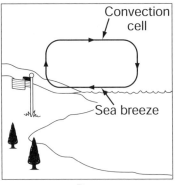

Day

At nighttime, the breeze changes direction. The land cools off faster than the water. The cooler inland air moves toward the warmer ocean air, creating a land breeze.

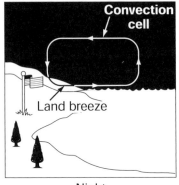

Night

Monsoon Winds

Monsoon winds are not local winds. However, they are winds that change direction because of the uneven heating of land and water. **Monsoon winds** are winds that change with the season. In India, for the six months between January and June, a dry land breeze blows from the northeast. In June, the wind reverses direction and brings moist ocean air to India. It happens suddenly, as soon as the land warms and air pressure drops. The moist ocean air brings with it a six-month rainy season.

Mountains and Valleys

The shape of Earth's landscape can also produce local winds. In mountainous regions, the mountains are first to receive the morning sunlight, starting an upward flow called a valley breeze. When night falls, the winds reverse and a mountain breeze blows down into the valley.

■ PRACTICE 25: Local Winds

Decide if each statement that follows is true (**T**) or false (**F**). Write the correct letter on each line.

_____ **1.** Water gets hot faster and cools off faster than land.

_____ **2.** Temperature change is moderate over a large body of water.

_____ **3.** The movement of ocean air toward the land is a sea breeze.

_____ **4.** There is a local high-pressure area over hot land during the day.

_____ **5.** Monsoon winds change direction twice each year.

_____ **6.** The daytime flow of air up a mountain is called a mountain breeze.

Planetary Winds

Where you live, winds change because of local conditions or because of the passing of high- and low-pressure systems. However, behind the scenes, another type of wind is at work. **Planetary winds** help circulate heat and moisture throughout the entire troposphere. Like all winds, planetary winds result from the uneven heating of Earth.

Planetary winds are created by uneven heating due to Earth's curvature. If Earth were flat, every location would collect the same amount of energy from the Sun. But, because of the curvature of Earth, solar energy is not collected evenly. The amount of energy a location collects changes with the latitude of the location. The latitude, measured in degrees, indicates how far north or south the location is from the equator.

The diagram below shows the Sun's rays striking the equator directly. North and south of the equator, the Sun's rays strike Earth at an angle. At the North Pole, the Sun's rays would just make it over the horizon. The same amount of solar energy is spread out over a larger area. Thus, the equator, and the regions surrounding it, collect more solar energy than the poles. At the equator, warm air rises, creating a band of low pressure. At the poles, cool, sinking air creates a high-pressure area.

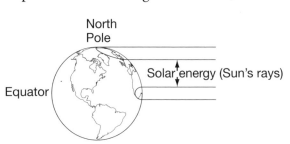

If Earth did not rotate, winds would circulate air between the low- and high-pressure areas at the equator and poles. On page 83, the diagram on the left shows how air would circulate through the troposphere on a non-rotating Earth. Air would rise at the equator and sink at the poles. The diagram on the right shows the actual pattern of planetary winds on Earth. The Coriolis effect causes the pattern of circulation to break apart. The winds circulate up and down through the troposphere in convection cells that mesh like gears.

Prevailing winds are the ground-level winds in the planetary wind system. They lie in wind belts across the globe. The prevailing winds between the equator and the 30° latitudes are called the northeast and southeast **trade winds.** The winds that carry weather systems across the United States are called the prevailing **westerlies.** Polar northeasterlies and polar southeasterlies are the winds that blow cold air from the poles.

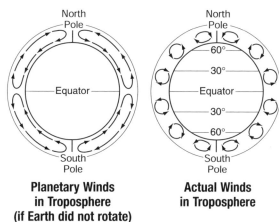

Planetary Winds in Troposphere (if Earth did not rotate)

Actual Winds in Troposphere

TIP

Wind is always named for the direction it comes from, not the direction it is heading toward. Thus, a *north wind* is a wind from the north that blows toward the south. The prevailing westerlies come from the west and blow toward the east.

Between the prevailing winds lie the pressure belts. Pressure belts are bands of high and low pressure. Low-pressure belts form where prevailing winds come together and the air is forced to rise. High-pressure belts form where the air is sinking. The **doldrums** is one of the low-pressure belts at the equator. The air in the doldrums is hot and humid, and slowly rising. There is little or no wind. Late afternoon showers form almost every day from the rising, moist air.

At the 30° latitudes, dry air sinks to form high-pressure belts called the horse latitudes. The dryness of the air may be one reason why there are so many deserts along the horse latitudes. The low-pressure areas at the 60° latitudes are called the subpolar lows. At the poles, cold, sinking air creates areas of high pressure called polar highs.

Just as local winds are affected by the landscape, so are the planetary winds. Earth's oceans, continents, and mountains each affect the patterns of wind and pressure belts. Wind and pressure belts in the north and south vary somewhat and shift with the seasons.

Jet Streams

The **jet streams** are strong rivers of wind that flow through the upper troposphere. They are the result of pressure gradients well above ground level. The path of a jet stream varies with the season, but in general, flows from the west toward the east. With wind speeds of over 300 kilometers per hour, the polar jet stream over the United States can help eastward-flying airplanes fly faster. Planes heading west avoid the jet stream.

■ PRACTICE 26: Planetary Winds

Decide if each statement that follows is true (**T**) or false (**F**). Write the correct letter on each line.

_____ **1.** The amount of solar energy a location collects changes with the latitude of the location.

_____ **2.** The Coriolis effect does not affect the pattern of planetary winds.

_____ **3.** Prevailing winds are ground-level winds.

_____ **4.** The trade winds carry weather systems across the United States.

_____ **5.** Wind is always named for the direction it is heading toward.

_____ **6.** At the equator, the air is dry.

_____ **7.** The jet streams are winds in the upper troposphere.

_____ **8.** The polar jet stream can help eastward-flying and westward-flying planes fly faster.

LESSON 8: The Changing Weather

 GOAL: To understand how weather systems form and why weather changes

WORDS TO KNOW

air mass	hurricane	temperate
climate	ice age	thunder
cold front	lightning	thunderstorms
continental air mass	low-pressure areas	tornado
El Niño	maritime air mass	tropical air mass
eye	occluded front	tropical depression
front	polar air mass	tropical storm
global warming	squall line	warm front
high-pressure areas	stationary front	wind shear

Air Masses

From studying the winds, it may seem that air is always on the move within the atmosphere. But in polar and tropical regions, large bodies of air may not move for weeks. When they do, they pick up the characteristics of the region. A large body of air that has nearly the same temperature, pressure, and humidity throughout is called an **air mass.** If air stays over the warm ocean for a few weeks, it will become a warm, humid air mass. If air spends time over cold land, it will become a cold, dry air mass.

Air masses are named for the area where they form. A **continental air mass** is one that forms over land. A **maritime air mass** forms over water. If the land or water lies in regions that are warm, such as the tropics, a **tropical air mass** is formed. A **polar air mass** is formed if the land or water lies in regions that are cold. The table that follows gives some information about each type of air mass. In parentheses are the abbreviations used on weather maps by meteorologists.

Type of Air Mass	Where Air Mass Formed	Properties of Air Mass
Continental Tropical (cT)	formed over land in hot areas near the tropics	hot, dry air masses that form in the summer over southwestern deserts
Continental Polar (cP)	formed over land in cold areas at higher latitudes	cold, dry air masses that move down from Canada
Maritime Tropical (mT)	formed over water in hot areas near the tropics	hot, moist air masses that can move in from either the Pacific Ocean or the Atlantic Ocean
Maritime Polar (mP)	formed over water in cold northern areas	cold, moist air masses that can move in from either the Pacific Ocean or the Atlantic Ocean

TIP

Maritime means "of the sea." The root of the word is *mare*, Latin for *sea*.

Polar and tropical air masses get set in motion when they overlap into the middle latitudes. The United States is a meeting ground for cold polar air and warm tropical air. The weather changes often, sometimes going from one extreme to the other. The map on the right shows the typical flow of air masses across the United States.

When an air mass moves into an area, it brings air of a certain temperature and humidity. The actual

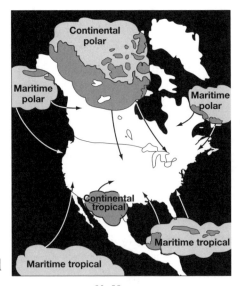

Air Masses

weather conditions depend on the temperature of the ground beneath the air mass. When a tropical air mass moves over colder land, the air cools from the bottom up. A temperature inversion occurs. Air will not rise, and smog can build up. The clouds are stratus-type, and often fog develops. If a polar air mass moves over warmer land, warm rising air produces cumulus clouds and clear air.

■ PRACTICE 27: Air Masses

Decide if each statement that follows is true (**T**) or false (**F**). Write the correct letter on each line.

_____ **1.** Air masses form over the United States.

_____ **2.** An air mass that formed over cold water would be abbreviated as mP.

_____ **3.** The weather changes often in the United States because polar and tropical air meet there.

_____ **4.** When a warm air mass moves over cold land, a temperature inversion occurs.

Fronts, Lows, and Highs

The boundary between two air masses is called a **front.** On a weather map, fronts are drawn as lines with semicircles or triangles along them. However, fronts are really surfaces that extend up through the troposphere.

If a warm air mass moves more quickly than a cold air mass, the boundary will be a **warm front.** The warm air mass rises over the cold air mass, giving a warm front a long sloping surface. You can tell from the clouds when a warm front is on the way. As the front moves in, high cirrus clouds will first appear, giving way to cirrostratus and altostratus

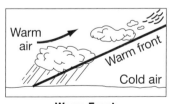

Warm Front

clouds. Eventually, nimbostratus clouds arrive, bringing steady rain or snow. After the front passes, temperatures will be warmer.

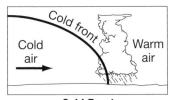

Cold Front

If the cold air mass moves more quickly than the warm air mass, the boundary will be a **cold front**. The cold air pushes up against the warm air, giving a cold front a steep surface. Warm air rises sharply at the front, producing cumulonimbus clouds. In a severe cold front, there will be a thunderstorm, with high winds and heavy rain or hail. Cold fronts pass through quickly, bringing cooler air in behind them.

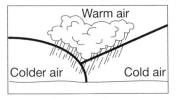

Occluded Front

Sometimes a cold front catches up to a warm front. The result is an **occluded front,** where a warm air mass becomes wedged between two cold air masses. When an occluded front moves in, cirrus clouds give way to layered stratus clouds, as in a warm front. When the cold front arrives, rain falls from cumulonimbus clouds. There may be very little change in temperature.

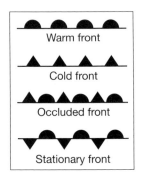

**Weather Map
Front Symbols**

Every so often, air masses do not move. The boundary between the cold air mass and the warm air mass is called a **stationary front.** A stationary front does not last long. Eventually, it changes into a warm or cold front.

Low-pressure areas develop along fronts when two air masses come together. Most low-pressure areas develop along the polar front, where cold polar air meets warm tropical air. The northern polar front falls across the mid-latitudes and is often over the United States. The exact location of the polar front changes with the seasons and is influenced by the jet stream.

Sometimes a wave or kink develops along the polar front. You can see how this happens in the diagram to the right. On one side of

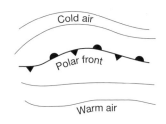

the wave, cold polar air pushes ahead and a cold front develops. On the other side of the wave, warm tropical air pushes ahead and a warm front develops. The warm air pushing forward is an area of lower pressure. The lowest pressure is at the crest of the wave. Winds circle around this low-pressure center in a counterclockwise direction. When a low-pressure area moves into your area, you can be sure of rainy or snowy weather.

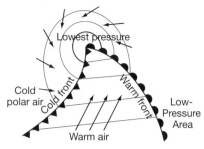

High-pressure areas do not form along boundaries of air masses. Instead, it is the air mass itself that is the high-pressure area. Often, there is a small pressure gradient across a high-pressure area. The winds that blow outward are not as strong as in a low-pressure area, and the weather is generally calmer and skies are clearer.

Determining exactly how the weather will change each day is the work of weather forecasters. When weather forecasters make their predictions, they look at all the factors you have learned: temperature, humidity, pressure gradients, and the prevailing winds. They determine how fast the fronts move, and they locate the jet stream and the polar front. Weather forecasters also check air temperature at ground level and at higher altitudes to determine how stable the air is. Even with all the data, weather forecasting is an imperfect science. Weather in the atmosphere is an extremely complex system.

THINK ABOUT IT

In the weather map on the right, what types of fronts are shown around the low-pressure area? What other types of fronts are shown on the map? How have the clouds and precipitation 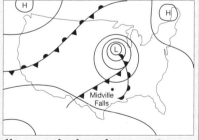 likely changed in Midville Falls over the last day or so? What do you forecast for Midville Falls in the near future? Write your answer on a separate sheet of paper.

■ PRACTICE 28: Fronts, Lows, and Highs

Look at the list of words below. Fill in each line with the letter of the correct word.

_____ 1. forms when two air masses do not move

_____ 2. brings nimbostratus clouds and rain or snow

_____ 3. forms along fronts

_____ 4. brings thunderstorms and cooler air

_____ 5. generally brings clear skies and a low-pressure gradient

_____ 6. where most low-pressure areas develop

_____ 7. forms when a cold front catches up to a warm front

a. warm front

b. cold front

c. occluded front

d. stationary front

e. polar front

f. low-pressure area

g. high-pressure area

Storms

Thunderstorms

Two thousand thunderstorms are in progress at any given moment. **Thunderstorms,** the most common of all storms, are storms formed of cumulonimbus clouds. These storms include thunder, lightning, heavy rain, and sometimes hail. Thunderstorms can occur either in the middle of an air mass or along a cold front. In both cases, warm, moist air rises through a deep layer of cooler, unstable air. When the moisture in the air condenses, the cloud front moves rapidly upward through the unstable air.

Cold-front thunderstorms are organized in a line called a **squall line.** This squall line runs ahead of the cold front. Cold-front thunderstorms may last for several hours, depending on the speed of the cold front. Afterward, the air is noticeably cooler and drier. An air mass thunderstorm occurs in the middle of an air mass in the late afternoon, when the ground is at its hottest. Most of these storms are short-lived.

After the storm, the temperature will not have changed. But it may be less humid.

Inside the cumulonimbus clouds are strong updrafts and downdrafts. The violent motion inside the cloud causes static electrical charges to build up and separate. Eventually, the cloud discharges, sending a stroke of static electricity, or **lightning,** to the ground. You may also see lightning when the charges leap from one part of the cloud to another.

The **thunder** in a thunderstorm is the sound of the air expanding as lightning burns a path through it. Sound waves travel more slowly than light waves, so you always see lightning before you hear thunder, unless you are directly under the storm.

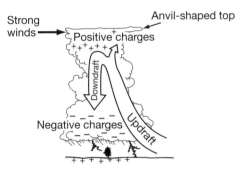

Thunderstorm

 TIP

Since lightning takes the shortest path to the ground, you should never take cover under a tree, or any tall object, during a thunderstorm.

Tornadoes

A **tornado** is produced by the most severe cold-front thunderstorm. Sometimes, winds will blow across the top of a cumulonimbus cloud in one direction and across the bottom in another direction. This is called **wind shear.** A rising updraft in the cloud can begin spinning because of wind shear. The spinning updraft turns into a tornado when it drops down from the bottom of the cloud and touches the ground. If there is a good chance that a tornado will develop, meteorologists will issue a tornado watch. A tornado warning means a tornado has already been spotted. The safest place to go during a tornado is to a basement or cellar.

Tornado

Winds in a tornado can reach up to 800 kilometers per hour. These intensely powerful storms are usually less than half a kilometer wide. They travel across the land at speeds between 40 and 72 kilometers per hour. Most tornadoes last only a few minutes, traveling about 6 kilometers before they break apart.

Certain parts of the country are likely locations for tornadoes to occur. In the central United States between March and May, cold, dry air masses push their way south and meet up with warm, wet air masses. The cold fronts that form are breeding grounds for severe thunderstorms and tornadoes.

Hurricanes

Hurricanes are different from thunderstorms and tornadoes. They are not formed along a cold front. Instead, a **hurricane** is an intense low-pressure area. The low-pressure center of a hurricane develops in the same way as other low-pressure centers. However, instead of forming along the polar front, hurricanes form over warm tropical waters at the equator, where the trade winds meet.

A hurricane usually begins as a small **tropical depression** in the South Atlantic. Warm, moist air rises and condenses to form cumulonimbus clouds. Winds swirl around the center of the hurricane in a counterclockwise direction. When wind speeds reach 65 kilometers per hour, the tropical depression becomes a **tropical storm.** When winds reach 118 kilometers per hour, the tropical storm is upgraded to a hurricane. Inside a hurricane, warm, moist air spirals upward around the center. The center of a hurricane is called the **eye.** The eye is an area with blue skies and light winds. Bands of cumulonimbus clouds collect around the eye, forming the eye wall. The strongest winds are near the eye. The average hurricane covers an area about 485 kilometers across.

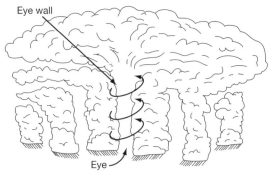

Hurricane

Where does a hurricane get its energy? It comes from the moisture condensing within the hurricane. Whenever water vapor condenses into water droplets, heat energy is released. Thus, with more condensation, more and stronger updrafts can develop, producing extremely high-speed winds. As long as the hurricane stays over warm waters, there is a ready supply of moisture to feed it. It will grow stronger until it travels over colder water or makes landfall. Hurricanes usually travel northwest, carried by the trade winds. Once a hurricane comes far enough north, it will be blown east by the prevailing westerlies. Hurricanes are a threat to the southeast coast of the United States in late summer and early fall.

■ PRACTICE 29: Storms

Decide if each statement that follows is true (**T**) or false (**F**). Write the correct letter on each line.

_____ **1.** Air mass thunderstorms are organized in a squall line.

_____ **2.** Lightning is seen when a cumulonimbus cloud discharges.

_____ **3.** Tornadoes may form if there is wind shear in a cumulonimbus cloud.

_____ **4.** Most tornado watches are issued between May and September.

_____ **5.** Hurricanes are cold-front storms.

_____ **6.** A hurricane's energy comes from the condensation of moisture within it.

Climate and Climate Change

When there are record-breaking high temperatures in July, are they due to the climate or the weather? Weather is the day-to-day change in the temperature, rainfall, air pressure, humidity, and winds in your area. Climate is the overall average weather of the area. Chances are, the record-breaking temperatures are simply related to the specific weather conditions that day. The two main considerations used to define the climate of an area are average annual temperature and average annual rainfall.

Climate Controls

Six climate controls affect temperature and rainfall. Latitude is the major controlling factor in determining the climate in an area. Tropical locations near the equator are hot and humid, while polar locations are cold and dry. Altitude also plays a role. Air is cooler and drier at higher altitudes. Prevailing winds will determine what kind of air mass reaches an area. The prevailing westerlies bring maritime air masses to the west coast, but primarily continental air masses to the east coast. Ocean currents, like the Gulf Stream, carry tropical water to northern latitudes and help keep temperatures warmer than expected.

IN REAL LIFE

To understand how ocean currents affect climate, just look at El Niño. **El Niño** is a periodic warming of ocean waters off the coast of Peru. During an El Niño year, the climate in Peru changes from dry to wet. The rains that fall are so heavy that they cause flooding and mud slides.

In general, locations near the ocean have cooler summers and warmer winters due to the high specific heat of water. Mountains can control climate by blocking winds that carry cold air or high humidity. Often, rains will fall on the windward side of a mountain. The other side of the mountain stays drier.

One way to classify world climates is to use average temperature and rainfall data. The climate map on page 95 divides Earth into three temperature zones: polar—below freezing most of the year; tropical— above 27°C most of the year; and **temperate**—with average temperatures in between. Also shown on the map are data on average annual rainfall. Areas can be either dry, moderate, or wet, as shown. The vegetation found in each climate area has adapted to grow given the climate type and the physical makeup of the land. You can use the climate map to find the general climate of an area. For example, San Diego, California, lies within a dry region in the tropical zone. Its climate is tropical dry.

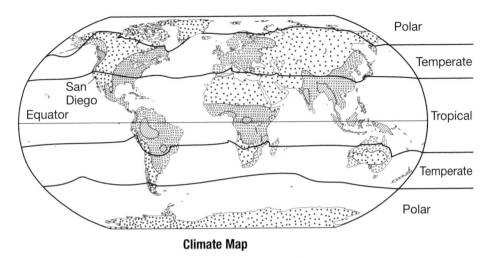

Climate Map

Average Annual Rainfall	
Dry (under 50 centimeters)	▓▓
Moderate (50–203 centimeters)	▒▒
Wet (over 203 centimeters)	▨

Average Annual Rainfall

Climate	Vegetation
polar dry climate	tundra; very little vegetation
polar moderate*	forests
temperate dry	vegetation varies widely; in United States, grasslands and deserts; in Canada and Asia, evergreen forests; in Southwestern Africa and Australia, deserts
temperate moderate	woodland; mostly deciduous trees
temperate wet	evergreen forests and deciduous trees
tropical dry	deserts (cactus)
tropical moderate	tropical forests and grasslands
tropical wet	tropical rain forests

*Since polar air is so dry, very few regions have a *polar moderate climate.* There is no such thing as a *polar wet climate.*

Climate Change

Even though you hear a lot about climate change today, it is nothing new. In the last 800,000 years, Earth has experienced at least four ice ages. During the last **ice age,** which ended 10,000 years ago, temperatures were cold enough for much of Earth's water to become frozen into glaciers. Sea levels were about 91 meters lower than they are now. Glaciers covered Canada and most of the northern United States. Yet, the average air temperature was 10°C—just 5°C cooler than it is today. The temperature change that led into, and brought Earth out of, the ice age occurred naturally and slowly over many thousands of years.

Today, we are in a natural period of temperature increases, or **global warming,** between ice ages. While Earth was heading into an ice age, it was experiencing a natural period of global cooling. There are many natural causes for global temperature change. Dust from volcanic eruptions can block the Sun. Energy received from the Sun can vary slightly. Natural events can control the amount of greenhouse gases in the air. Today, when climate scientists talk about global warming, they are referring to the risk of rapid, unnatural temperature change that is a result of human activities.

Global warming is linked to increasing levels of carbon dioxide in the atmosphere. Carbon dioxide is released during the burning of fossil fuels, such as oil, gas, and coal. Before 1900, few fossil fuels were burned, and carbon dioxide levels stayed constant. Since then, as shown on the graph on the top right, carbon dioxide levels have been increasing along with the burning of fossil fuels.

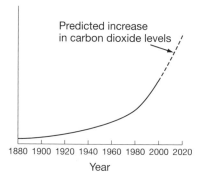

In the graph on the bottom right, you can see that Earth's average temperature varies from year to year. However, since about 1925, there has been a steady rise

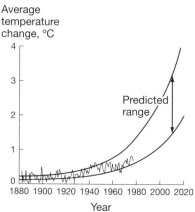

in temperatures. Is the burning of fossil fuels the leading cause? Most climate scientists agree that it is. The graphs include a range of predictions for the future. According to these predictions, average global temperatures are expected to go up anywhere from 1.5° to 2.5°C by the year 2025. Carbon dioxide levels are expected to increase as well.

THINK ABOUT IT

Use the climate map on page 95 to determine the climate in your area. Write your answer on a separate sheet of paper if needed.

Many scientists are afraid that the rate of change in global temperatures will be too fast. Polar ice will melt, and sea levels will rise. Coastal communities will be washed away. World climates will change. The vegetation of an area may not be able to adjust to the rapid climate change. It is unclear how animals and humans will adjust.

Not all scientists are in agreement about how fast temperatures will rise. Nobody can predict exactly how climates will change. However, because of this concern, countries are joining together to reduce fossil fuel use. Alternative energy sources, conservation, and recycling are all possible solutions. Small efforts, like planting a tree, can also help. Trees absorb carbon dioxide and help clear the atmosphere. Helping to keep the atmosphere clean is just part of the regular maintenance of Earth's life support system.

■ PRACTICE 30: Climate and Climate Change

Decide if each statement that follows is true (**T**) or false (**F**). Write the correct letter on each line.

_____ **1.** The two main factors that influence climate are average annual temperature and rainfall.

_____ **2.** Latitude, altitude, and ocean currents are examples of climate controls.

_____ 3. Scientists are worried about global warming because there has never been any climate change in Earth's history.

_____ 4. Carbon dioxide levels have been increasing since humans started burning fossil fuels.

_____ 5. During the ice ages, sea levels were higher.

UNIT 2 REVIEW

Circle the answer that correctly completes each of the following statements.

1. The gases most important to weather and climate are
   _____.
   a. uniform gases
   b. variable gases
   c. nitrogen and oxygen

2. All of Earth's weather happens in the _____.
   a. troposphere
   b. stratosphere
   c. thermosphere

3. The air particles in the atmosphere are mainly heated by the Sun's energy that is _____.
   a. absorbed by the ground
   b. absorbed by the atmosphere
   c. absorbed and reemitted by the ground

4. Areas of low pressure on a weather map are most likely
   _____.
   a. cold and dry
   b. warm and humid
   c. located in mountainous regions

5. Closed curves on a weather map are called _____.
    a. isobars
    b. millibars
    c. low-pressure centers

6. _____ clouds form in a deep layer of unstable air.
    a. Nimbostratus
    b. Cumulonimbus
    c. Cumulus

7. _____ are created by uneven heating on Earth's surface.
    a. Planetary winds
    b. Winds in high- and low-pressure areas
    c. All winds

8. Planetary winds are caused by _____.
    a. the Coriolis effect
    b. uneven heating of land and water
    c. uneven heating owing to Earth's curvature

9. When a warm air mass moves more quickly than a cold air mass, the boundary will be _____.
    a. a cold front
    b. a warm front
    c. an occluded front

10. Wind shear in a cumulonimbus cloud can lead to _____.
    a. hail
    b. tornadoes
    c. hurricanes

UNIT 2 APPLICATION ACTIVITY 1
Heating Earth's Surface

The atmosphere around Earth greatly affects the temperature of Earth. Here is a way to demonstrate the effect of atmosphere on temperature.

Using equal amounts of dry soil, fill two containers of equal sizes to within 1 or 2 cm of the tops. Place a thermometer in the soil of each container so that the bulb of each thermometer is just below the surface.

Place both containers under a heat lamp for ten minutes. The temperature of the soil in each container at the end of ten minutes should be 15° to 20°C higher than room temperature.

Leave the thermometers in place, and turn off the heat lamp. Immediately place plastic wrap over the first container, and secure it tightly. Leave the second container uncovered.

Record the starting temperatures at time 0—the time at which you turned the lamp off—in the chart. Observe and record the temperature of the soil in each container every minute for 15 minutes.

Time (min.)	Temperature Uncovered (°C)	Temperature Covered (°C)
1		
2		
3		
4		
5		
6		
7		
8		
9		
10		
11		
12		
13		
14		
15		

Plot your data as a graph in the space below. Use the graph on the right as a sample. You can vary the scale depending upon your results.

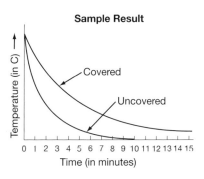

Sample Result

Temperature (in C) →

Covered

Uncovered

0 1 2 3 4 5 6 7 8 9 10 11 12 13 14 15
Time (in minutes)

1. Did both containers of soil absorb the same amount of energy from the heat source?

   _____

2. Which container had the least temperature change in 15 minutes? Why? _____

   _____

   _____

   _____

   _____

3. How is your model similar to real Earth and its atmosphere? How is it different? _____

   _____

   _____

   _____

   _____

   _____

UNIT 2 APPLICATION ACTIVITY 2

The Weight of Air

Have you ever wondered how much air weighs? Try making your own barometer to find out.

Inflate a balloon, and then deflate it. Cut the neck of the balloon as shown in the diagram on the right. Stretch the balloon over the open end of a coffee can. Use a rubber band to hold the balloon tightly in place. Glue one end of a broom straw to the center of the balloon. Be sure the straw extends about 10 centimeters past the rim of the can.

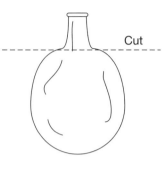

Fold an unlined sheet of paper as shown in the diagram below. Make marks about 0.5 cm apart along the central fold. Write numbers that increase from the bottom up next to your marks. Note that the numbers on the scale are arbitrary. Write "high pressure" at the top of the scale and "low pressure" at the bottom. As air pressure changes, the balloon cover will rise or fall. The broom straw will point to different spots on the scale.

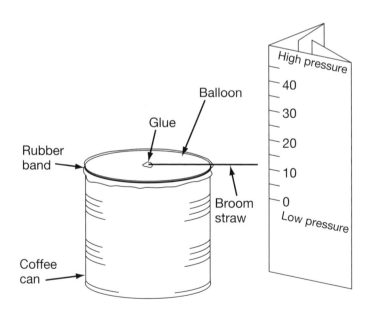

Record the air pressure indicated by your barometer daily for one week. Record it in the chart below. Also record the weather conditions.

1. What change in the atmosphere must occur in order for the broom straw to rise?

_____

_____

_____

2. What change must occur for the straw to lower?

_____

_____

_____

3. What kind of weather occurs with high pressure?

_____

_____

_____

4. What kind of weather occurs with low pressure?

_____

_____

_____

	Day 1	Day 2	Day 3	Day 4	Day 5	Day 6	Day 7
Pressure							
Weather conditions							

UNIT 3

The Ground Beneath Us

LESSON 9: What Is Planet Earth?

GOAL: To become familiar with Earth's structure and ways to map its surface

WORDS TO KNOW

continental crust	magnetic declination	outer core
contour lines	magnetosphere	parallels
crust	mantle	polyconic projection
degrees	map projections	prime meridian
elevation	map scale	radioactive decay
inner core	Mercator projection	silicates
isolines	meridians	topographic
latitude	minutes	true north
longitude	oceanic crust	

Earth's Surface and Interior

Suppose you could view Earth from the Moon. To you, Earth would seem like a smooth, round, slowly spinning sphere. In fact, Earth is not a sphere. Because Earth spins, it bulges slightly at the equator. At the poles, Earth's diameter is 12,714 kilometers. But at the equator, Earth's diameter measures 12,757 kilometers—just 43 kilometers more.

Why, then, does Earth seem smooth? After all, its highest mountain, Mt. Everest, rises to a height of 8850 meters above sea level. Earth's deepest valley is called the Mariana Trench. It drops to a depth of 11,033 meters below sea level. However, compared to the size of Earth, these are but tiny ripples on the surface.

IN REAL LIFE

If Earth were the size of an apple, then Mt. Everest would be a tiny bump 0.025 millimeters high. It would be too small for you to even notice!

Inside Earth

The outer surface of this huge spinning planet is the ground you walk on. Where the ground meets air, all forms of life can be found. But Earth's surface only tells part of the story. Geologists are scientists who study the ground beneath us. They have discovered that Earth's surface is the top of a thin outer crust. This thin **crust** is the first of four layers inside Earth.

How do geologists know what is inside Earth? The deepest mines only scratch the surface of Earth's crust. To find out what is inside, geologists study the vibrations set off by earthquakes. Earthquake waves travel through Earth. When these waves reach a layer of different material, some of them are bent, while others are slowed down. Geologists have learned the thickness, composition, and temperature of Earth's four layers by comparing data collected from earthquakes all over the world.

The crust covering Earth is so thin that if Earth were an apple, the crust would be about the same thickness as the apple's skin. There are 90 naturally occurring elements on Earth. Only eight of these make up 98.5% of Earth's crust. These elements are oxygen, silicon, aluminum, iron, calcium, sodium, potassium, and magnesium. These elements join together to form the minerals and rocks that make up Earth's crust.

The crust is thinnest, but densest, beneath the oceans. This **oceanic crust** is between 4 and 10 kilometers thick. It consists mainly of a type of rock called basalt. **Continental crust,** the crust below Earth's land masses, is thicker, but lighter, than oceanic crust. It sinks deeper into the layer below (the mantle), but also rises higher above it. Continental crust can range anywhere from 35 to 70 kilometers in depth. Granite and rocks similar to granite make up most of the continental crust. Below the top 20 meters, temperatures within Earth increase. Where the crust meets the next layer (the mantle), the temperature is about 500°C.

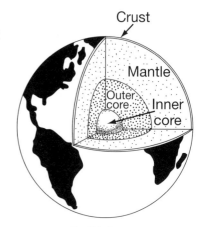

Earth's Layers

Beneath the crust is Earth's biggest layer, the mantle. The mantle is about 2900 kilometers thick. It is made up mainly of minerals called silicate minerals. Silicates are composed of metals, silicon, and oxygen. Some examples are quartz, feldspar, micas, garnet, and talc. Temperatures rise to 3000°C in the lower mantle. The mantle is plastic, meaning it can move slowly. You will learn more about moving rocks in Lesson 11, page 133.

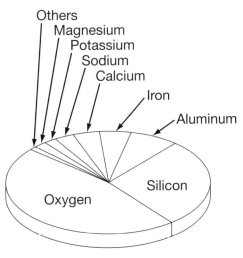

Composition of Earth's Crust

Beneath the mantle is the outer core. The outer core is Earth's only liquid layer. It is made of nickel, iron, and possibly several other elements. The outer core is about 2300 kilometers thick. Where the outer core meets the inner core, temperatures are believed to be 3600°C. In the center of Earth is the inner core. The inner core is a solid metal sphere made of iron and nickel. It is about 2700 kilometers in diameter and extremely hot. Temperatures at the center of Earth are believed to be 4500°C. The inner core stays solid because of the intense pressure bearing down on it.

Why Earth Has Layers

Geologists believe that Earth's layers separated because of their different densities. Shortly after Earth formed, 4.6 billion years ago, it was bombarded with meteorites. The impact of the meteorites created enough heat to melt some of Earth's rocks. Once these rocks melted, the densest materials sank deep into Earth's center. This is what formed the core. The lighter materials floated to the top, forming the crust. The mantle, in between the crust and the core, formed from what was left.

Earth's Internal Heat

The high temperatures inside Earth come from several sources. Since Earth is slow to cool off, it still contains heat from the impact of meteorites long ago. Also, friction from movement within the crust creates heat. Finally, some heavy elements found in the rocks are slowly decaying, or breaking down, into lighter, more stable elements. This process is called **radioactive decay.** As the elements decay, they also give off heat. However, Earth is not getting hotter. The heat created inside Earth is balanced by the heat escaping to the outside through volcanoes, geysers, and hot springs.

■ PRACTICE 31: Earth's Surface and Interior

Decide if each statement that follows is true (**T**) or false (**F**). Write the correct letter on each line.

_____ **1.** Earth's diameter is 12,757 kilometers greater at the equator than at the poles.

_____ **2.** Geologists study earthquake waves to learn what is inside Earth.

_____ **3.** Continental crust is thicker and lighter than oceanic crust.

_____ **4.** The mantle is the thinnest layer of Earth.

_____ **5.** The outer core is Earth's only liquid layer.

_____ **6.** Geologists believe that Earth had separate layers from the start.

_____ **7.** High temperatures inside Earth are due entirely to radioactive decay.

Earth as a Magnet

Earth behaves as if there is a huge bar magnet running right through its center. Like a bar magnet, Earth has magnetic poles. Earth is also surrounded by a magnetic force field. This force field is called the **magnetosphere.** The motion of iron within the liquid outer core is believed to be the cause of Earth's magnetic field. When you hold a magnetic compass in your hand, the needle lines up with the magnetosphere. One end points toward the magnetic north pole. The other end points toward the magnetic south pole. As a result, you can use a compass to get you pointed in the correct direction.

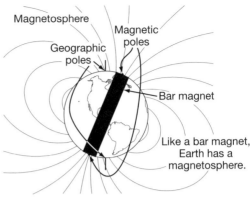

Earth's Magnetic Field

However, if you were to rely completely on a compass for navigation, you would likely get lost. That is because a compass needle points toward magnetic north, not true north. **True north** is located at the geographic North Pole. It is one end of the imaginary axis on which Earth rotates. Magnetic north is located about 1600 kilometers away from the geographic North Pole, near Canada. Magnetic south is in Australia, about 1600 kilometers from the geographic South Pole. The difference between true north and magnetic north is called **magnetic declination.** Magnetic declination varies depending on where you are. Some maps include the area's magnetic declination so that compass readings can be adjusted.

Every few million years, Earth's magnetic field completely reverses itself. The north magnetic pole becomes the south magnetic pole, and the south magnetic pole becomes the north magnetic pole. Currently, the south magnetic field is actually near the geographic North Pole. Geologists are not certain why this happens. However, the fact that it does happen has proved useful, as you will see in Lesson 11, page 133.

■ PRACTICE 32: Earth as a Magnet

Decide if each statement that follows is true (**T**) or false (**F**). Write the correct letter on each line.

_____ **1.** A compass needle points to true north.

_____ **2.** Earth has a magnetosphere because of motion within the liquid outer core.

_____ **3.** Magnetic declination is the difference between true north and magnetic north.

_____ **4.** Earth's magnetic field reverses itself every 100 years.

Earth as a Globe

Have you ever bought a ticket to a large sporting event? There may be thousands of seats in the stadium. But, with the row number and seat number on your ticket, you have all the information you need to find your seat. Latitude and longitude are like the row number and seat number for Earth's surface. They help you find your place on the round globe. **Latitude** is the distance in degrees of any point north or south of the equator. **Longitude** is the distance in degrees of any point east or west of the prime meridian (defined on page 113). Together, latitude and longitude lines create a grid system that covers the entire globe.

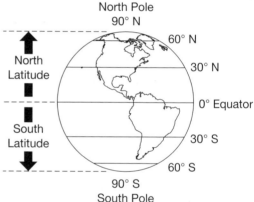

Latitude lines, also called **parallels,** are imaginary rings that circle the globe. These lines run parallel to the equator. The equator has a latitude of 0°. Locations north of the equator have a north latitude. Locations south of the equator have a south latitude. The North Pole has a latitude of 90° N (north). The South Pole has a latitude of 90° S (south).

Longitude lines, also called **meridians,** are imaginary half-circles that run east and west of the prime

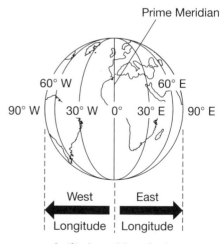

Latitude and Longitude

meridian. The **prime meridian** runs from the North Pole to the South Pole through Greenwich, England. It has a longitude of 0°. If you move away from the prime meridian, the farthest you can go is 180° E (east) or 180° W (west).

You have learned that latitude and longitude lines are expressed in **degrees.** For greater precision, degrees are divided into 60 smaller units called **minutes.** (Minutes can be further divided into 60 smaller units called seconds.) For example, Chicago, Illinois, has a north latitude of 41 degrees and 50 minutes, or 41° 50' N, and a west longitude of 87 degrees and 37 minutes, or 87° 37' W. You can see Chicago on the map on the right. The latitudes and longitudes of some other major cities are given on page 116.

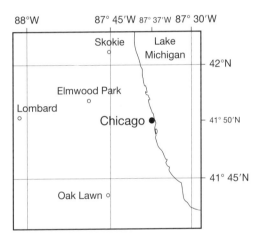

Since latitude lines are parallel, the distance between them stays the same everywhere. For all locations, one degree of latitude equals 112.7 kilometers, and one minute of latitude equals 1.88 kilometers. Longitude lines, on the other hand, get closer together the farther they are from the equator. Thus, the distance between longitude lines does not stay the same. At the equator, a degree of longitude is about the same as a degree of latitude.

■ PRACTICE 33: Earth as a Globe

Decide if each statement that follows is true (**T**) or false (**F**). Write the correct letter on each line.

_____ **1.** Longitude is the distance in degrees of any point east or west of the prime meridian.

_____ **2.** Latitude lines are also called meridians.

_____ **3.** For greater precision, a degree is divided into 60 minutes.

_____ **4.** Locations halfway around the world from the prime meridian have a longitude of 180°.

_____ **5.** One degree of longitude stays the same everywhere.

Mapping Earth

When it comes to mapping Earth, Earth's shape causes problems. There is no easy way to show all of a round Earth on a flat sheet of paper. Most world maps you have seen are actually map projections. **Map projections** show the globe or an area on it as it would appear projected onto a flat surface. There are many different ways to make map projections. None of them is perfect. One of the ways, called the **Mercator projection,** is the one with which you are probably most familiar. On a Mercator projection, meridians become parallel lines. The distance between latitude lines increases away from the equator.

Mercator Projection

The Mercator projection works well for mid-latitudes. But for high latitudes, distance is greatly distorted. For example, Greenland appears to be the same size as Africa. But, in fact, it is about half the size of Australia, which is much smaller than Africa. All world map projections have some distortions. However, maps of smaller areas are more accurate. The most accurate projection for small areas is called the **polyconic projection** (seen on the right).

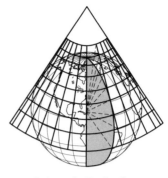

Polyconic Projection

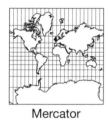

Mercator

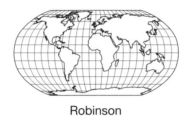

Robinson

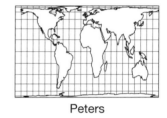

Peters

Three Map Projections

Maps are always much smaller than the areas they show. Thus, most maps have a map scale. A **map scale** shows how map distance compares to actual distance. Map scales are created in two different forms. One is a comparison of how many centimeters on the map equals an actual number of kilometers. For example, "1 centimeter = 10 kilometers." The second is a graphic drawing like the one below.

0   10 km

Look at the list of locations and their latitudes and longitudes. Then look at their position on the map, which is a Mercator projection. In finding the distance between two places on this type of map, does a map scale work? Explain.

City	Latitude	Longitude
San Diego, CA	32° 42' N	117° 10' W
New York City, NY	40° 47' N	73° 58' W
Rio de Janeiro, Brazil	22° 57' S	43° 12' W
Dakar, Senegal	14° 40' N	17° 28' W
London, England	51° 32' N	0° 5' W
Moscow, Russia	55° 45' N	37° 36' E
Bombay, India	19° 0' N	72° 48' E
Tokyo, Japan	35° 40' N	139° 45' E
Sydney, Australia	34° 0' S	151° 0' E

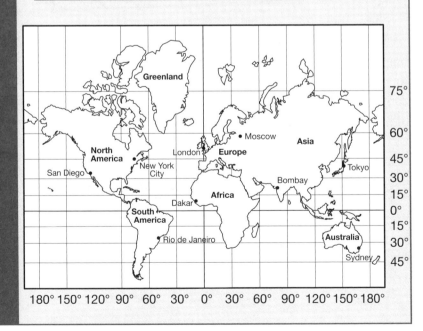

Topographic Maps

If you wanted information about how the landscape changes from hills to valleys, you would use a topographic map. **Topographic** maps are particularly useful for hikers and climbers who want to know the steepness of the trail in front of them. Most topographic maps are polyconic projections.

The United States Geological Survey (USGS) makes topographic maps for all regions of the United States. **Elevation,** or the height above sea level, is measured throughout the entire region and placed on a map. Then lines are drawn that connect points of equal elevation. The lines are called **isolines** or **contour lines.** When drawing the map, the mapmaker would choose a contour interval. The contour interval is the difference in elevation between each contour line. A typical contour level would be 6 meters. In addition, the mapmaker would label the elevation on every fifth contour line. On the map below, you can see that contour lines never cross one another.

Topographic maps, or contour maps, are similar to the pressure maps you learned about in Unit 2. Pressure maps show lines of equal pressure. On a pressure map, you can see how quickly pressure changed by looking at how close together the isobars are. On a contour map, you can tell how steep the land is by looking at how close together the contour lines are. The closer the lines, the steeper the hill. On the map to the right, the steepest part is between points B and C. There, the contour lines are close together. Between points A and B, there is a gentle hill. Notice that points A and D have the same elevation.

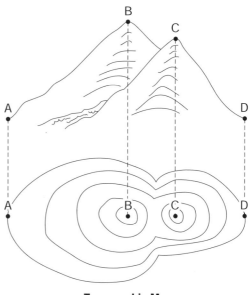

Topographic Map

The series of V-shaped contour lines between points B and C show the location and path of a river running through the area. Rivers always run downhill, and the V shapes in the contour lines always point upstream. On all USGS topographic maps, you will find a map scale, magnetic declination for the area, longitude and latitude marks, and a key to all symbols used.

■ PRACTICE 34: Mapping Earth

Look at the list of terms below. Write the letter of the correct term on the line before each description.

_____ 1. used to make contour maps

_____ 2. shows contour lines

_____ 3. shows direction a river flows

_____ 4. show areas that are steep

_____ 5. distorts distance at high latitudes

_____ 6. shows difference in elevation between contour lines

_____ 7. another name for contour lines

_____ 8. a way of showing a round Earth on a flat surface

_____ 9. height above sea level

_____ 10. shows how map distance compares to actual distance

a. map projection

b. contour interval

c. polyconic projection

d. Mercator projection

e. close contour lines

f. V-shaped contours

g. map scale

h. isolines

i. topographic map

j. elevation

LESSON 10: Within the Crust

 GOAL: To become familiar with the minerals, rocks, and fossil fuels in Earth's crust

WORDS TO KNOW

basalt

batholith

calcite

chemical sedimentary
  rocks

clastic

cleavage

coal

conglomerate

contact metamorphism

crystal

crystalline solid

dike

erosion

extrusive rocks

felsic magma

fossil fuels

fracture

gabbro

gemstones

gneiss

granite

hydrocarbons

igneous

inorganic

intrusive rocks

laccolith

lava

limestone

luster

mafic magma

magma

marble

metals

metamorphic

mineral ore

obsidian

organic

petroleum

porous rock

pumice

quartzite

regional
  metamorphism

renewable resources

rhyolite

rock cycle

sandstone

sedimentary

shale

silica

sill

slate

specific gravity

streak

weathering

Minerals

What are minerals? There is no one common look or use of a mineral. Minerals can be **gemstones,** such as diamond and ruby, or **metals,** such as gold, silver, and copper. You can eat some minerals, such as halite, also known as salt. **Calcite** is a mineral used in toothpaste and medicines. Gypsum is used to make plaster. Aluminum is a metal used for everything from soda cans to house gutters. It comes from bauxite, a **mineral ore.** An ore is any rock or mineral that contains a valuable metal. Other minerals, such as feldspar, mica, and quartz, come together to form rocks.

There are over 3000 different minerals found in Earth's crust. They can form from evaporation of hot fluids, or from heat and pressure within Earth. There is enormous variety among the minerals. So, what is it that makes a mineral a mineral? All minerals share the following four properties.

- All minerals are made of one or more key elements combined in a specific way. Based on the elements in the mineral, a mineral can be described as either native, silicate, or nonsilicate. There are about 50 native minerals, each made from a single element. Many metals, such as gold and silver, are native minerals. Diamond is also a native mineral, made from the single element carbon. There are over 500 silicate minerals made from the elements silicon and oxygen. Most rocks in Earth's crust are made from silicate minerals. All other minerals fall under the broad category of nonsilicate minerals.

- All minerals are natural. Minerals are used in synthetic materials. But synthetic materials are not minerals themselves. Glass has quartz in it, but it is synthetic. Therefore, glass is not a mineral.

- All minerals are inorganic. For a material to be **inorganic,** it must not be made of living things. For example, seashells and pearls are not minerals. This is because they are parts of mollusks and marine animals. But they are made of a mineral—calcite.

- All minerals are crystalline solids. In a **crystalline solid,** the atoms arrange themselves in a regular pattern. As the mineral forms, the pattern repeats itself. The geometric shape that results is called a **crystal.** There are six main crystal systems, shown on page 121. If grown under different conditions, the same elements can produce different crystals. Both diamond and graphite are made from the element carbon. Yet, diamond is clear and hard. Graphite is dark and soft. The difference is due to their internal shapes, or crystals.

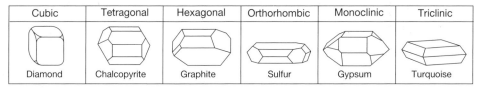

Cubic	Tetragonal	Hexagonal	Orthorhombic	Monoclinic	Triclinic
Diamond	Chalcopyrite	Graphite	Sulfur	Gypsum	Turquoise

Examples of Crystal Systems

Identifying Minerals

Now that you know how to tell if a material is a mineral, you need to learn how to tell one mineral from the next. There are eight simple tests that are used to help identify minerals. These are shown in the table below.

	What to Look for in a Mineral
Color	May not be useful since many minerals have the same color.
Crystal shape	May be difficult to notice since crystals can be very small.
Luster	Describes how light reflects from a mineral; can be dull, metallic, pearly, glassy, greasy, or silky.
Hardness	Resistance to being scratched, based on Mohs' scale of hardness. On Mohs' scale, ten common minerals are ranked between 1 and 10. Talc, the softest mineral, is ranked 1. Diamond, the hardest mineral, is ranked 10. Higher ranked minerals will scratch lower ranked minerals. With a series of scratch tests, the hardness of any mineral can be found.
Streak	Color of mineral's powder when rubbed on a white tile; can be different from the mineral color.
Cleavage	Ability to split along flat surfaces; especially useful in identifying mica, a mineral made of paper-thin layers.
Fracture	Manner in which mineral breaks if there is no cleavage.
Specific Gravity	Density of mineral compared to water.

When you use a pencil, you are testing the streak of the mineral graphite. Graphite is the "lead" used in pencils.

A test that is useful for identifying the mineral calcite is the acid test. A drop of weak acid like vinegar will bubble and fizz when it touches calcite.

■ PRACTICE 35: Minerals

Decide if each statement that follows is true (**T**) or false (**F**). Write the correct letter on each line.

_____ **1.** All minerals have a common look.

_____ **2.** Gemstones are minerals.

_____ **3.** Most rocks are made of silicate minerals.

_____ **4.** Native minerals are made of living things.

_____ **5.** The same elements can produce different crystals.

_____ **6.** A very hard mineral would have a rating of 1 on Mohs' scale of hardness.

_____ **7.** Color is the most useful way to identify a mineral.

_____ **8.** The acid test is useful in identifying calcite.

_____ **9.** All minerals are crystalline solids.

_____ **10.** Luster describes the color of a mineral.

Igneous Rocks

Have you ever looked closely at a rock? In some rocks, you can see different minerals. Each mineral is a different color. All rocks are combinations of minerals bound together. The types of minerals in a rock, the size of the grains, and the way they are bound together are a result of how the rock was formed. Rocks can form in three different ways, resulting in either igneous, sedimentary, or metamorphic rocks.

IN REAL LIFE

It is easy to see the minerals bound together in a speckled rock such as granite. You probably have seen granite in a building foundation, curbstone, or just on the ground. Granite is one of the most common rocks on Earth's crust. It is made of coarse grains of three different colors. The dark grains are mica. The clear grains are quartz. The pink or white grains are feldspar.

Igneous rocks are formed from magma. **Magma** is hot melted rock inside Earth. When magma breaks through Earth's surface (is extruded), as in a volcano, the magma becomes **lava.** When lava cools, the resulting rocks are extrusive igneous rocks. Since they are exposed to the open air, **extrusive rocks** cool and harden quickly. The crystals, with little time to grow, remain small. As a result, extrusive igneous rocks are fine-grained.

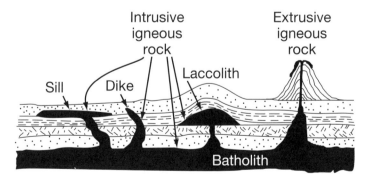

Igneous Rocks

Sometimes magma pushes upward but does not break through the surface. Instead, it collects underground, developing into one of four formations.

- a **dike**—when magma cuts up through layers of rock
- a **sill**—when magma cuts across layers of rock
- a **laccolith**—when magma bulges up to make a dome
- a **batholith**—when magma fills in a huge area deep underground

If the magma cools before ever reaching the surface, the rocks are called intrusive igneous rocks. **Intrusive rocks** cool very slowly and are coarse-grained. The hardened dikes, sills, laccoliths, and batholiths reach Earth's surface after the rock above has worn away.

All magma contains **silica,** a combination of the elements silicon and oxygen. These are the same elements found in the silicate minerals that form rocks. Magma with a low silica content is called **mafic magma.** It is dark, thin, and runny. Magma with a high silica content is called **felsic magma.** It is light-colored, thick, and pasty.

Examples of Igneous Rocks

Granite is an intrusive igneous rock made of felsic magma. It is the most common intrusive igneous rock. Granite is a coarse-grained rock containing the silicate minerals quartz, feldspar, and mica. The crystals within granite are locked together, making the stone very hard and strong. Because of its strength, granite is used in building foundations.

Rhyolite is an extrusive igneous rock also made of felsic magma. In fact, rhyolite has the same composition as granite. But it is glassy and fine-grained because it erupted from an explosive volcano. **Pumice** has the same composition as rhyolite but was made from a frothy and bubbly lava. The many pockets of air in pumice make it so light that it floats in water. **Obsidian** is a glassy extrusive rock that cooled so quickly no crystals could grow.

Basalt is an extrusive igneous rock made of mafic magma. Basalt is fine-grained and made from feldspar and augite, a dark mineral. Most volcanic lava is basalt. Basalt is the most common rock in Earth's crust. You may have seen these dark rocks used between railroad ties along railroad tracks.

Gabbro is an intrusive igneous rock also made of mafic magma. Its composition is about the same as basalt, but it is coarse-grained.

■ PRACTICE 36: Igneous Rocks

Decide if each statement that follows is true (**T**) or false (**F**). Write the correct letter on each line.

_____ **1.** Igneous rocks are made of magma.

_____ **2.** When lava cools, an intrusive igneous rock forms.

_____ **3.** A sill forms when magma cuts up through rock layers.

_____ **4.** A batholith forms when magma fills in a huge area deep underground.

_____ **5.** Magma with a low silica content is called mafic magma.

_____ **6.** Light-colored, thick, and pasty magma is mafic magma.

_____ **7.** An example of an extrusive igneous rock is basalt.

_____ **8.** A rock with many pockets of air is pumice.

Sedimentary Rocks

Have you ever noticed places on a highway where the road cuts through a hill, leaving cliffs on either side? These road cuts often reveal layer upon layer of long-buried rock. These rock layers are probably sedimentary rocks. **Sedimentary** rocks are formed from sediments cemented together in layers. Sediments can be grains of rock, pieces of shells, or dissolved minerals that settle to the bottom of water. As sediments are continually covered by new layers of sediment, they become deeply buried. Pressure squeezes the sediment, forcing out water and air bubbles. Many sedimentary rocks are then cemented together by naturally occurring cements.

Clastic Sedimentary Rocks

Clastic sedimentary rocks are formed from sediments made from bits and pieces of other rock. Rocks on the surface are constantly undergoing **weathering,** or the process of breaking apart, because of rain, wind, freezing, and thawing. Running water carries the sediments in streams toward a lake or an ocean. As the sediments rub against one another, they are eroded, or worn down. The sediments become smooth and rounded. When the stream reaches the lake or ocean, it slows down. Then the sediments are deposited. The largest pebbles settle first, followed by the smaller sand-sized grains. Tiny bits of clay and silt stay suspended longest. Finally, the clay and silt settle farthest from the stream.

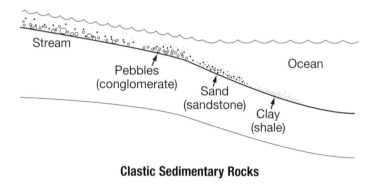

Clastic Sedimentary Rocks

Conglomerate contains the largest sediments—pebbles held together by cement. **Sandstone** is made of grains of sand cemented together. Most sand is the mineral quartz, which is hard and durable. If you scratch hard at sandstone, though, grains of sand can break off. **Shale** is made of tightly packed sediments of clay and silt. It is a dark, fine-grained rock.

Organic Sedimentary Rocks

Organic sedimentary rocks are formed from sedimentary remains of animals and plants. There are two main types of organic rock. These are limestone and coal. Organic **limestone** is formed from the shells of clams, oysters, and other shellfish that fall to the ocean floor. Like the shells, limestone is made of the mineral calcite. Limestone holds up well as a building material. The Great Pyramids in Egypt were made of limestone blocks 4500 years ago.

What could you use to test a rock to see if it is limestone?
Write your answer on a separate sheet of paper.

Coal is made from the remains of plants that were buried and compacted in swampy areas. Coal is mainly carbon, an element found in all living things. The carbon content of coal rises the longer the coal remains buried. There are four stages in the development of coal: peat, lignite, bituminous, and anthracite.

Anthracite is the hardest, most carbon-concentrated coal. When it is burned, anthracite releases the greatest amount of energy. The released energy is the energy absorbed by the plants millions of years ago.

Chemical Sedimentary Rocks

Chemical sedimentary rocks can form from the minerals left behind when ocean water evaporates. They can also form when dissolved minerals chemically combine and become solid. The solid sediment then collects on the ocean floor. Chemical limestone contains tiny grains of calcite that were dissolved in seawater. Rock salt is a chemical sedimentary rock made from the salt of dried-up oceans.

■ PRACTICE 37: Sedimentary Rocks

Decide whether each word below and on the next page is associated with clastic (A), organic (B), or chemical (C) sedimentary rocks. Write the correct letter on each line. (*Hint:* There may be more than one correct answer.)

_____ **1.** coal

_____ **2.** sandstone

_____ **3.** weathering

_____ **4.** sediments

_____ **5.** limestone

_____ **6.** rock salt

_____ **7.** shale

_____ **8.** layers

Metamorphic Rocks

One other type of rock is found on Earth's surface. These rocks are not created from magma or sediments. Instead, **metamorphic** rocks are created when igneous and sedimentary rocks are changed by intense heat and pressure inside Earth. Pressure makes the rocks squeeze together. Then they become more and more dense. Heat makes the minerals in a rock break down and rearrange themselves into new rocks. Since metamorphic rocks are created underground, they make their way to the surface only as the land above erodes. There are two ways that igneous and sedimentary rocks can change into metamorphic rocks.

TIP

Meta- means "change," and *morph* means "form." Thus, metamorphic rocks are rocks that have changed form.

One way that igneous and sedimentary rocks can change is regional metamorphism. **Regional metamorphism** occurs when large areas of rock are changed by heat and pressure. See the diagram below. These rocks form deep within the crust under mountain ranges. When mountains are created, pressure on the crust makes the rocks buckle and fold. The pressure, along with heat, changes the rocks into metamorphic rocks. When granite, an igneous rock, undergoes regional metamorphism, it changes into a rock called gneiss. **Gneiss** is called a high-grade regional metamorphic rock. Both pressure and temperature are extremely high when gneiss is formed. **Slate** is a low-grade regional metamorphic rock made when temperature and pressure are low. Slate comes from the

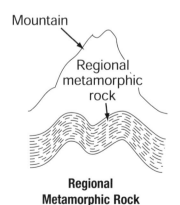

Regional
Metamorphic Rock

sedimentary rock shale. Chalkboards, roofing tiles, and patio stones can be made from hard and durable slate.

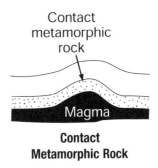

Contact metamorphic rock

Contact Metamorphic Rock

The second way that igneous and sedimentary rocks can change into metamorphic rocks is by contact metamorphism. **Contact metamorphism** occurs when hot magma bakes rocks that come in contact with it. This can happen when intrusive igneous rocks are formed. Contact metamorphism affects smaller areas of rock than regional metamorphism does. **Marble** is a contact metamorphic rock made from the sedimentary rock limestone. Like limestone, marble is made of calcite. Polished marble is used on floors and in buildings. **Quartzite** is a metamorphic rock made from sandstone, another sedimentary rock. It is a hard, dense rock that is used to make gravel.

The Rock Cycle

Over the course of Earth's long history, rocks in the crust have changed from one form to another in a process known as the **rock cycle.** Once they reach the surface, metamorphic, sedimentary, and igneous rocks are all

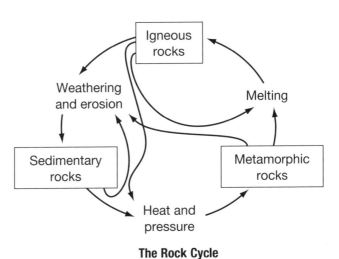

The Rock Cycle

subject to the forces of weathering and erosion that break down rock. **Erosion** is the removal of the products of weathering by any natural agent. The bits of rock become sediments that, over time, become sedimentary rocks. Sedimentary rocks changed by heat and pressure will become metamorphic rocks. If temperatures are high enough, any of the three rocks may melt into magma. When magma cools and hardens, igneous rocks are formed. The rock cycle is shown in the diagram above.

■ PRACTICE 38: Metamorphic Rocks

Decide if each statement that follows is true (**T**) or false (**F**). Write the correct letter on each line.

_____ **1.** Both igneous and sedimentary rocks can become metamorphic rocks.

_____ **2.** Contact metamorphism occurs when hot magma melts rocks.

_____ **3.** A low-grade regional metamorphic rock, such as slate, is made when heat and pressure are high.

_____ **4.** Marble is a high-grade regional metamorphic rock.

_____ **5.** Only igneous rocks weather.

_____ **6.** Rocks cycle through Earth's crust, changing to all three forms.

Petroleum and Natural Gas

Have you heard of fossil fuels? Coal, petroleum, and natural gas are all sources of energy called **fossil fuels.** As you learned before, coal is a sedimentary rock made from the remains of plants. It contains the element carbon. **Petroleum,** also called oil, is a liquid believed to be made from the remains of both plants and animals. The remains became buried in sediments in shallow ocean water. Like coal, petroleum formed over a long period of time as heat and pressure acted on the decaying matter.

TIP

The fuels are called *fossil* fuels because they are made from the remains of living things that died many years ago.

Natural gas is thought to have formed at the same time as petroleum, since it is often found in the same location. Both petroleum and natural gas contain hydrocarbons. **Hydrocarbons** are a combination of carbon and hydrogen. They are by-products of the decayed matter. When carbon and hydrocarbons are burned, they release large amounts of energy. This is why coal, petroleum, and natural gas are used as fuels.

When gas and petroleum first formed, they seeped upward through layers of porous rock above. **Porous rock,** such as sandstone, has tiny spaces between the grains. If groundwater fills the spaces, gas and petroleum rise above it. This is because they are lighter than the water. Natural gas, the lightest of all fossil fuels, rises above the petroleum. The gas and petroleum stop rising only if they reach a layer of rock that geologists call a trap. A trap is a layer of rock, such as shale, that is not porous. The grains in shale are so small that there is no space between them. Geologists look for traps when they hunt for oil and gas reserves.

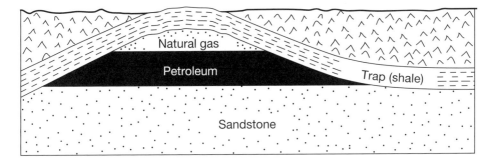

Natural gas and petroleum are trapped by
a nonporous trap like shale.

A Shale Trap

Energy Resources

The advantage of fossil fuels is the tremendous energy stored in an easily used material. The energy is used to drive cars, heat houses, produce electricity, and make many petroleum-based products. Unfortunately, burning fossil fuels releases carbon dioxide and other pollutants. The carbon dioxide contributes to the steady buildup of greenhouse gases in the atmosphere. The pollutants contribute to health problems, acid rain, and the thinning ozone layer.

In addition to these health and environmental problems, fossil fuels are nonrenewable resources. Their supplies are limited to what is on Earth now. The supply of coal is expected to last for another 250 years or so. Natural gas and petroleum supplies may run out in as little as 50 years.

Some alternative energy sources are wind power, water power, solar power, and geothermal power. They are clean **renewable resources,** or energy sources that can be replaced. However, none of these renewable energy resources can provide as much energy as easily as fossil fuels. Researchers continue to find ways to collect and store enough renewable energy to meet our society's needs.

■ PRACTICE 39: Petroleum and Natural Gas

Decide if each statement that follows is true (**T**) or false (**F**). Write the correct letter on each line.

_____ **1.** A fossil fuel made from plants and animals is petroleum.

_____ **2.** A fossil fuel that contains hydrocarbons is coal.

_____ **3.** Petroleum is heavier than water.

_____ **4.** A trap is a layer of nonporous rock.

_____ **5.** Fossil fuels are nonrenewable.

_____ **6.** The most energy that is easily available comes from solar power.

LESSON 11: Beneath the Crust

> **GOAL:** To understand the forces beneath the crust that create mountains, earthquakes, and volcanoes

WORDS TO KNOW

aftershocks	focus	rift zones
asthenosphere	fold mountains	seafloor spreading
caldera	hot spots	seismic waves
cinder cone	lithosphere	seismograph
composite cone	L wave	shield cone
cone	magma chamber	subduction zones
continental drift	Pangaea	S wave
dome mountains	plate tectonics	transform fault
earthquake	polarity	tsunami
epicenter	P wave	vent
fault	Richter scale	volcanic mountains
fault-block mountains	rift	volcanoes

Continental Drift and Seafloor Spreading

If the continents were puzzle pieces that could be moved around, South America and Africa would be an obvious fit. In 1915, a German scientist, Alfred Wegener, was the first to propose that South America and Africa actually did once fit together like puzzle pieces. In fact, he believed that all the continents were once attached in a giant super-continent called **Pangaea.** See the illustration on page 134.

Wegener came up with a theory that he called the theory of **continental drift.** It stated that Pangaea broke up millions of years ago, and the continents have been moving away from one another ever since. As evidence for his theory, Wegener noted that the same types of rocks and fossils were found in both western Africa and eastern South America. The

Pangaea 250 Million Years Ago   **The Continents 65 Million Years Ago**

evidence was not enough for most geologists of the time. They could not imagine a force strong enough to move the continents. Sadly, Wegener died before more evidence was found to prove him correct.

In the 1960s, evidence was found that supported the theory of continental drift. There is a huge underwater mountain range, called the Mid-Atlantic Ridge, running the entire length of the Atlantic Ocean. In the center of the ridge, scientists found a **rift,** or crack, in the crust. Magma poured out of the rift and hardened. It appeared as though new crust was forming along the rift. The older crust was pushed away to either side. This idea became known as **seafloor spreading.**

The most convincing evidence that the seafloor was spreading came from the magnetic properties of the seafloor rocks. While the rocks were still molten, magnetic materials within them lined up with Earth's magnetic field. The rocks hardened, locking in the **polarity,** or direction, of the magnetic field. The polarity of rocks near the rift showed the present polarity. Farther away, on either side of the rift, the polarity of the rocks was reversed. Still farther away, the polarity returned to normal. When geologists marked the magnetic reversals on a map (see map on the right), they made a pattern like zebra stripes.

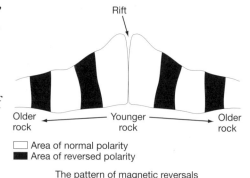

The pattern of magnetic reversals helped prove seafloor spreading.

Magnetic Reversals

How could this help prove seafloor spreading? Remember that every few million years, Earth's magnetic field reverses itself. The pattern in the rocks showed that newly made ocean crust pushed aside the older crust.

The seafloor was spreading apart and pushing the continents away from one another. Geologists today accept the idea of Pangaea. They agree that South America was once connected to Africa, as Wegener had proposed. The Atlantic Ocean is growing an inch wider each year, and has been growing for the last 200 million years!

■ PRACTICE 40: Continental Drift and Seafloor Spreading

Decide if each statement that follows is true (**T**) or false (**F**). Write the correct letter on each line.

_____ **1.** Alfred Wegener believed that the continents are drifting together and will someday form a super-continent called Pangaea.

_____ **2.** The Mid-Atlantic Ridge is an underwater mountain range.

_____ **3.** Seafloor spreading refers to weathering and erosion of the Mid-Atlantic Ridge.

_____ **4.** Evidence for seafloor spreading came from the pattern of magnetic reversal in the rocks.

_____ **5.** At a rift, newly made ocean crust pushes aside older crust.

Plate Tectonics

Continental drift and seafloor spreading led geologists to a new view of Earth's outer layers. Today, geologists call the crust and rigid upper mantle the lithosphere. The solid lithosphere is about 100 kilometers thick. It is broken into pieces called plates. The plates rest on top of a layer within the mantle called the asthenosphere. The rocks of the asthenosphere are plastic, which means they move slowly. High temperatures and pressure allow the rocks to flow. Heat inside Earth causes the rocks to slowly rise and fall on giant convection currents. The convection currents drive the movement of Earth's plates. The study of Earth's moving plates is called plate tectonics.

The lithosphere is broken into eight large plates and several smaller plates. These plates fit together like a jigsaw puzzle. The plates move slowly, at about the same

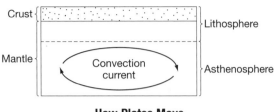

How Plates Move

rate as your fingernails grow. Motion of one plate affects all of the plates. As you can see from the maps below, most earthquakes and volcanoes are found along plate boundaries. Many mountain ranges are also found along plate boundaries. Stresses build along the boundaries as the plates either move apart, move together, or slide past one another.

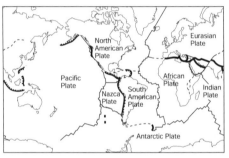
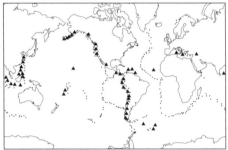

— Collision zone
⌇⌇ Subduction zone
— Transform fault
= Rift zone
--- Uncertain boundary

▲ Volcanoes
⋰ Earthquakes

Plate Tectonics

A **fault** is any crack in the crust where there is movement. A **transform fault** happens when plates slide past each other. You have probably heard of the San Andreas Fault in California. Most of California lies on the North American Plate. But a small part of southern California lies on the Pacific Plate. The Pacific Plate is slowly sliding to the northwest. Many earthquakes result as the plates grind past each other.

At **rift zones,** plates move slowly apart from each other. Along the resulting gap, magma can rise to the surface. New crust is created and added to the edge of the plate. The Mid-Atlantic Ridge is an example of a rift zone.

Where one continental plate meets another continental plate, it is called a collision zone. At **subduction zones,** old crust is destroyed as it plunges down into the mantle. If a plate carrying oceanic crust collides with a plate carrying continental crust, the denser oceanic plate subducts, or sinks beneath, the lighter continental plate. An example of this type of subduction zone is along the west coast of South America. There, the Nazca Plate sinks beneath the South American Plate. The edge of South America has crumpled into a long mountain range called the Andes Mountains. There are many volcanoes within the Andes Mountains. Subduction also occurs when two oceanic plates collide. As one plate is forced beneath the other, a deep trench forms. You will find most volcanoes along subduction zones.

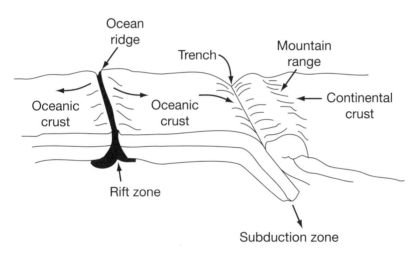

Examples of Faults

THINK ABOUT IT

By looking at the map on page 136, can you see why the edge of the Pacific Ocean is often referred to as the "Ring of Fire"? Write your answer on a separate sheet of paper.

■ PRACTICE 41: Plate Tectonics

Look at the list of terms below. Write the letter of the correct term on the line before each description.

_____ 1. the crust and upper mantle

_____ 2. plates rest upon this layer

_____ 3. the study of moving plates

_____ 4. where plates slide past each other

_____ 5. where continental plate meets continental plate

_____ 6. where continental plate meets ocean plate

_____ 7. a crack in the crust at which there is movement

_____ 8. where most earthquakes, volcanoes, and mountain ranges form

_____ 9. where plates move apart

a. subduction zone

b. collision zone

c. rift zone

d. plate boundaries

e. plate tectonics

f. asthenosphere

g. lithosphere

h. fault

i. transform fault

Volcanoes

Earth used to be covered by volcanoes. **Volcanoes** are openings in the ground from which magma flows. In the years after Earth formed, volcanoes were a way for the planet to release the tremendous amount of heat inside. Today, there are about 30 volcanic eruptions each year that still serve the same purpose—to allow heat trapped beneath the crust to escape.

When a volcano erupts, layers of lava build up to form a **cone.** Magma pours out of a **vent** through the cone. Beneath the volcano, a pocket of hot magma collects in a **magma chamber.** Sometimes after an eruption, when the magma chamber is emptied, the top of the cone collapses. The resulting crater is called a **caldera.** Crater

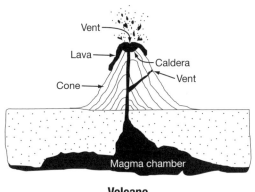

Volcano

Lake in Oregon is a caldera. It sits over an inactive volcano that filled in with rainwater. Calderas also form as a result of explosive eruptions.

Not all volcanoes are explosive. The amount of gas in the magma when the volcano erupts will determine whether the eruption is explosive or gentle. Magma deep underground contains gases that are trapped due to the high pressure. Most gases escape as the magma rises and pressure is reduced. The amount of gas that can escape will depend on the thickness of the magma. The thickness of the magma is determined by the amount of silica in the magma.

Low-silica magma, called mafic magma, is dark, thin, and runny. Gases escape easily because the magma is so thin. The resulting lava usually erupts gently and flows smoothly. However, if mafic magma rises too quickly, less gas can escape. Then the lava sprays from the volcano in a fiery fountain. Water can also mix with mafic magma to produce fiery eruptions. Two different types of mafic lava are the rough-surfaced aa and the ropy-textured pahoehoe. Most mafic magma produces the volcanic rock basalt.

High-silica magma, called felsic magma, is light-colored, thick, and pasty. Gases cannot escape as easily because the magma is so thick. The trapped gases produce explosive eruptions. The lava that hardens quickly is called tephra. Tephra comes in all sizes. Tiny pieces are called ash, pea-sized pieces are called lapilli, and the largest pieces are called bombs. The rocks rhyolite and pumice are formed from explosive eruptions of felsic magma.

Types of Eruptions

Subduction zone eruptions are explosive. Volcanoes form when pressure underground forces magma to break through the surface. The cone that forms can be either a composite cone or a cinder cone. Both are steep. A **cinder cone** is formed from ash and cinders. A **composite cone** has layers of ash and lava. The Cascade Range in the Pacific northwest region was formed along a subduction zone. One of the mountains, Mt. St. Helens in Washington state, was an example of a steeply sided composite cone before it exploded in 1980. See the diagram on the right. When pressure built up inside the volcano, the entire northwest side of the mountain was blown away. The caldera that resulted is over 3 kilometers wide.

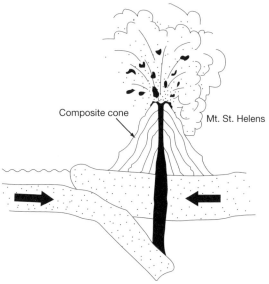

Subduction Zone Eruption

Hot spot eruptions have produced the chain of Hawaiian Islands. **Hot spots** are areas of intense heat within the asthenosphere that can burn holes through the lithosphere. Mafic magma rises up through the hole and builds a wide **shield cone** with gently sloping sides. The hot spot that formed the Hawaiian Islands is in the middle of the Pacific Plate. See the diagram below. The Pacific Plate is like a slow-moving conveyor belt. As it moves northwest, it carries one island off the hot spot, making way for a new island to form. The process has created a long chain of islands. The big island of Hawaii now sits over the hot spot and is the only island with active volcanoes.

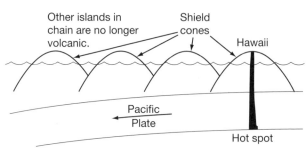

Formation of Hawaiian Islands

Rift zone eruptions do not form cones and are not explosive. Eruptions along the rift zone in the mid-Atlantic have formed the Mid-Atlantic Ridge. When the mafic lava erupts, it cools quickly and hardens to create new ocean crust. Most of the oceanic crust is made of the igneous rock basalt, formed from mafic lava along rift zones.

■ PRACTICE 42: Volcanoes

Decide if each statement that follows is true (**T**) or false (**F**). Write the correct letter on each line.

_____ **1.** Magma pours out of a vent.

_____ **2.** Felsic magma produces explosive eruptions.

_____ **3.** Mafic magma produces ash.

_____ **4.** Explosive eruptions are found at rift zones.

_____ **5.** Shield cones form at subduction zone eruptions.

Earthquakes

You probably never thought of rocks as elastic. But rocks, like rubber bands, will stretch when pulled hard enough. The force that can stretch rocks is friction between lithospheric plates trying to grind past each other. Like rubber bands, rocks will reach a point where they can stretch no more. Further pulling breaks the hold, letting the plates slip past each other. The rocky crust breaks violently, causing a wave of energy to shake the ground above. This shaking of the ground is called an **earthquake.**

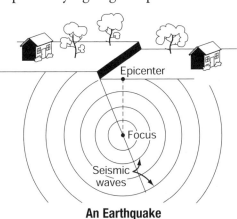

An Earthquake

Earthquakes occur underground at a point called the **focus.** Directly above the focus on the surface is the **epicenter.** Earthquakes can happen along any fault or plate boundary. Often they occur before or after a volcano erupts. Earthquakes with the deepest focus are found along subduction zones where one plate is sinking deep into the mantle. Rift zones and transform faults, such as the San Andreas Fault, produce shallower earthquakes. See the diagram on page 141.

Seismic Waves

When there is an earthquake, the rebounding rocks send out waves of energy in all directions. These **seismic waves** come in three forms. The first type of seismic wave is the primary or **P wave.** P waves are compression waves, like sound waves. The ground moves back and forth along the direction of travel. P waves are the fastest earthquake waves and can travel through any material, even air.

The second type of seismic wave is the secondary or **S wave.** The S wave moves the ground at right angles to the direction of travel. S waves are slower than P waves and are not carried through liquid. Thus, S waves are stopped by the liquid outer core. When the S and P waves reach the surface, they create the third type of seismic wave, called a surface wave or **L wave.** Surface waves move the ground up, down, and sideways. They are the slowest of all.

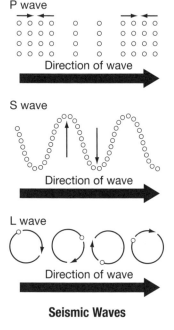

Seismic Waves

■ IN REAL LIFE

People who have experienced a major earthquake recall hearing a roaring sound as the earthquake struck. The roar was produced when P waves traveled right out of the ground and into the air. In air, some P waves become low-frequency sound waves.

When seismic waves pass through a city, the damage can be devastating. Buildings collapse because foundations are unable to withstand the shaking. Gas mains and electrical connections can break, causing fires. Often an area will be hit with **aftershocks** that shake the ground for several days afterward. If the earthquake's epicenter is underwater, nearby coastal areas may be hit by a tidal wave, or **tsunami.** In open water, a tsunami is a long, low wave that travels quickly. When it reaches shallow water, the wave rises high out of the water and causes considerable damage on shore.

Earthquake waves can be measured by an instrument called a **seismograph.** A seismograph can record either horizontal or vertical motion. During an earthquake, a seismograph pen will record the seismic waves on a rotating drum. First the P waves, then the S waves, and finally the L waves are recorded. Seismologists then compare the data collected from seismographs around the world. The timing and size of the waves can reveal the time, location, and size of the earthquake. It was through analysis of seismic waves that geologists learned about the structure of Earth's layers.

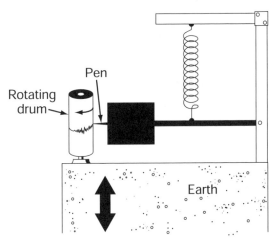

Vertical Motion Seismograph

You may have heard news reports that mention the strength of an earthquake as a number on the **Richter scale.** The Richter scale was developed by American seismologist C. F. Richter to compare the sizes of earthquakes in California. Earthquakes with a rating of 1 on the Richter scale are felt only by instruments. The strongest earthquakes ever recorded have a rating between 8 and 9 on the Richter scale. These earthquakes have destroyed buildings, bridges, and roads.

On Sunday, December 26, 2004, a tsunami struck coastlines in countries along the Indian Ocean. More than 140,000 people were killed in Indonesia, Sri Lanka, India, Thailand, and several other countries. The huge wave was created by an earthquake in the Indian Ocean. The earthquake measured 9.0 on the Richter scale and struck at 7:00 A.M. The wave, which was as large as 14 meters (40 feet) tall, began to hit coastlines $\frac{1}{2}$ hour after the earthquake. It finally lost its momentum along the east coast of Africa.

In both the Pacific Ocean and the Indian Ocean, there are sensors that tell researchers when and where an underwater earthquake hits. And for the countries that border the Pacific, there is an early warning system for tsunamis. This warning system allows research stations around the Pacific to warn Pacific Rim governments when a tsunami is likely to hit. The governments have signals in place to get their residents away from the coasts. Because of the devastation caused by the 2004 tsunami, governments around the Indian Ocean are pushing for a similar early warning system.

■ PRACTICE 43: Earthquakes

Decide if each statement that follows is true (**T**) or false (**F**). Write the correct letter on each line.

_____ **1.** An earthquake happens when plates slide past or under each other, breaking the rocky crust.

_____ **2.** Earthquakes with the deepest epicenter are found along subduction zones.

_____ **3.** The fastest seismic wave is the P wave.

_____ **4.** Surface waves are stopped by the liquid outer core.

_____ **5.** If the earthquake epicenter is underwater, a tsunami may form.

_____ **6.** Seismographs record seismic waves.

_____ **7.** The stronger the earthquake, the higher its number on the Richter scale.

Mountains

The same forces that produce earthquakes and volcanoes have produced some of Earth's tallest mountains and longest mountain ranges. Some mountains are still being made, like the Himalayas in Nepal. Others, like the Appalachians in the eastern United States, were made when Pangaea formed. Many young mountain ranges are still forming along subduction and collision zones. Mountains can be made in four different ways.

■ All mountain ranges of the world are **fold mountains.** Whenever plates collide, the rigid crust buckles and folds as if it were made of clay. The process that builds mountains takes place over millions of years. The Indian Plate first made contact with the Eurasian Plate 40 million years ago. Moving at a rate of about 2.5 cm a year, the Indian Plate has pushed forward to create a ridge of folded crust. This ridge of folded crust is the Himalayan Mountain range.

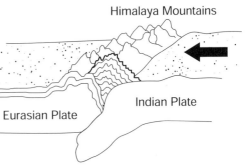

Fold Mountains

The Himalayas are considered a young mountain range because they are still forming. They grow about half a centimeter each year. The Appalachian Mountains, on the other hand, are an old mountain range. They were created because the African Plate collided with the North American Plate when Pangaea was formed. Possibly the Appalachian Mountains were once as large as the Himalayas. But they stopped growing 250 million years ago when Pangaea broke apart. Since then, they have been slowly worn down by weathering and erosion.

- **Fault-block mountains** form when one block of land is forced up above another. Pressure on colliding plates can produce cracks or faults in the crust. Along these faults, the crust can split into blocks. The continued pressure produces fault-block mountains. Weathering wears down the edges and covers the fault. The Sierra Nevada Mountains in California are an example of fault-block mountains.

- **Volcanic mountains** are cone-shaped mountains built up from layers of lava. Often, volcanic mountains are found along subduction zones. Mt. St. Helens in the Cascade Range is an example. Volcanic mountains are also found in the Andes Mountains in South America.

- **Dome mountains** can form from a laccolith when magma pushes up, but does not break through, Earth's crust. The ground above the laccolith bulges upward, creating a dome-shaped mountain. Dome mountains, such as the Henry Mountains in Utah, do not form long mountain chains.

TIP

Weathering and erosion go on everywhere on Earth all the time. Even the Himalayas are breaking down. However, they are building up faster than they are eroding.

■ PRACTICE 44: Mountains

Decide if each statement that follows is true (**T**) or false (**F**). Write the correct letter on each line.

_____ **1.** The Himalayas are an example of fault-block mountains.

_____ **2.** Long mountain chains are fold mountains.

_____ **3.** The Henry Mountains in Utah are dome mountains.

_____ **4.** Mountains that form over laccoliths are volcanoes.

LESSON 12: Earth's History

GOAL: To understand how Earth's history is hidden in rocks

WORDS TO KNOW

absolute age	half-life	radiometric dating
carbon dating	index fossils	relative age
epochs	mineral cast	superposition
eras	mineral mold	trace fossils
fossils	mineral remains	trilobites
geologic timetable	periods	uranium dating

The Fossil Record

When Alfred Wegener proposed the theory of continental drift, he used fossils as evidence. **Fossils** are any evidence of past plant or animal life found in rocks. Geologists use fossils to piece together Earth's history. The best place to look for fossils is in sedimentary rocks. When plants and animals die, their bodies may end up buried in sediment. Over time, as the sediments change to rock, the plants or animals change to fossils.

THINK ABOUT IT

Why are igneous or metamorphic rocks not good places to look for fossils? Write your answer on a separate sheet of paper.

There are four ways that fossils can form.

- **Trace fossils** are impressions left by plants and animals. An impression would be the imprint of a leaf or the footprint of a dinosaur.

Leaf imprint

Trace Fossil

- Sometimes, the original remains of an animal are found. Usually, original remains are bones, teeth, or other hard parts. Original remains of an entire woolly mammoth, including soft parts, have been found frozen in glaciers. Insects were preserved when they became trapped in sticky sap. The sap later hardened into a clear yellow rock called amber.

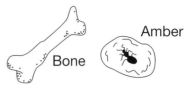

Original Remains

- If mineral-rich water seeps slowly into the body of a plant or an animal, the fossil may end up as **mineral remains.** The soft parts decay. Minerals in the water replace the hard parts bit by bit. The resulting fossil is the hardened mineral that has taken on the shape of the plant or animal. Petrified wood is an example of mineral remains.

Mineral Remains

- Sometimes, the original remains decay completely, leaving a hole in the rock. The hole has the original shape of the plant or animal and is called a **mineral mold.** If minerals fill in the mold, they form a hard **mineral cast.** Both molds and casts have been found of trilobites. **Trilobites** are hard, crablike sea creatures believed to be one of the earliest animals to have lived on Earth. Trilobite fossils are very old.

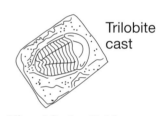

Mineral Cast or Mold

Geologists view each fossil that they find as another clue to the mystery of the past. For geologists to use fossils, they must know how old a fossil is compared to other fossils. They rely on the law of **superposition.** This law states that in undisturbed rock layers,

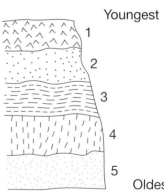

Superposition

the oldest rock is always on the bottom. Geologists have to be careful in using this law. Rock layers can be overturned. Or, a layer of magma may have squeezed between existing layers and hardened into a layer of igneous rock.

Based on the law of superposition and the fossils found within each layer, geologists have put together a sequence of plants and animals that lived in the past. This sequence gives the relative age of the fossils, from oldest to youngest. A fossil's **relative age** is its age compared to the other fossils in the sequence. The actual age of a fossil is called the **absolute age.** You will learn about methods of finding absolute age on page 150.

Certain fossils can be used as index fossils. **Index fossils** are fossils of animals that lived for a short time throughout a wide part of the world. Trilobites meet these criteria and make good index fossils. If a trilobite is found within a layer of rock, geologists know the relative age of that layer. It is the same as the relative age of all other rock layers with trilobites.

■ PRACTICE 45: The Fossil Record

Look at the list of terms below. Write the letter of the correct term on the line before each description.

_____ 1. evidence of past life

_____ 2. best rock to look for fossils

_____ 3. imprint of a leaf

_____ 4. woolly mammoth frozen in glacier

_____ 5. minerals replace hard parts

_____ 6. minerals fill in mold

_____ 7. one of earliest animals on Earth

_____ 8. oldest rocks are on bottom layer

_____ 9. used to find relative age of a rock layer

_____ 10. actual age of rocks

a. trilobite

b. trace fossil

c. cast

d. sedimentary

e. fossil

f. index fossil

g. original remains

h. mineral remains

i. absolute age

j. law of superposition

Radiometric Dating

To measure the absolute age of Earth's rocks, geologists use radiometric dating. **Radiometric dating** relies upon the rate of decay of radioactive elements. As you learned in Lesson 1, radioactive elements decay to lighter, more stable elements. The rate of decay is measured in terms of half-life. **Half-life** is the time it takes for half of the element to decay, or change, into a more stable element. The shorter the half-life, the faster the decay rate of the element.

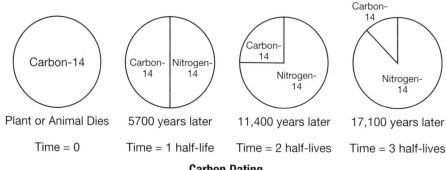

| Plant or Animal Dies | 5700 years later | 11,400 years later | 17,100 years later |
| Time = 0 | Time = 1 half-life | Time = 2 half-lives | Time = 3 half-lives |

Carbon Dating

Carbon dating is useful in finding the age of plants and animals. Carbon-14 is a part of all living things. As soon as a plant or an animal dies, carbon-14 begins to decay. The half-life of carbon-14 is about 5700 years. It takes 5700 years for half of the carbon-14 to decay into nitrogen-14, a stable element. After another 5700 years, half of what was left has decayed. Every 5700 years, half of the remainder decays. Carbon dating can be used until the amount of carbon-14 is too small to measure. For most plants and animals, this is about 100,000 years. Scientists can find the age of a fossil by comparing the amount of carbon-14 to the amount of nitrogen-14.

However, carbon dating cannot be used on rocks that do not contain fossils or are older than about 100,000 years. Another element, uranium-238, is useful in finding the age of Earth's oldest rocks. It has a half-life of 4.5 billion years. Geologists can find the age of almost any rock formed within Earth's 4.6 billion year history by using uranium-238 (**uranium dating**) and several other radioactive elements with shorter half-lives.

The Geologic Timetable

Radiometric dating provides a way to learn about Earth's past by using the rocks and fossils of the present. The **geologic timetable,** shown on page 215 in Appendix C, summarizes Earth's geologic history. It was created by using absolute and relative ages of fossils and rocks found throughout Earth's crust. On the geologic timetable, Earth's past has been divided into four major **eras.** Each era can be further divided into **periods.** (Periods can be divided into **epochs,** not shown in the table.) The divisions in Earth's history are linked to the major forms of life found in each era.

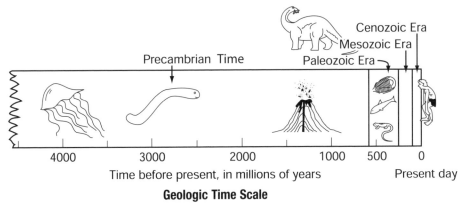

Geologic Time Scale

The time of modern humans—the last 11,000 years—
is too small to show on the geologic time scale.

IN REAL LIFE

Did you ever see the movie *Jurassic Park* or its sequels? The movies are about dinosaurs brought to life in modern times. The series takes its name from the Jurassic period.

As you can see from the table on page 215, life on Earth has changed many times over its history. Changes take place gradually over many millions of years. They do not happen suddenly. Why have some species died out and others become dominant? Climate change may be one factor. Dinosaurs may have been victims of climate change. They are thought to have become extinct after an asteroid struck Earth 65 million years ago. Dust from the impact blocked sunlight, killing first the plants, then the plant-eating dinosaurs, and finally, the meat-eating dinosaurs.

Human presence on Earth is but a tiny fraction of Earth's long history. How long will humans last? Will climate change be the end of the age of mammals? Nobody can say for sure. However, it can be said with certainty that planet Earth will continue to gradually but steadily change as it travels into the future.

■ PRACTICE 46: Radiometric Dating

Circle the answer that correctly completes each of the following statements.

1. To measure absolute age of Earth's rocks, geologists use _____.
   a. the geologic timetable
   b. radiometric dating
   c. both *a* and *b*

2. The shorter the half-life, the _____.
   a. faster the decay rate
   b. slower the decay rate
   c. both *a* and *b*

3. As soon as a plant or an animal dies, the element that begins to decay is _____.
   a. carbon-14
   b. nitrogen-14
   c. uranium-238

4. The "Age of Mammals" is _____.
   a. the Cenozoic Era
   b. the Mesozoic Era
   c. the Paleozoic Era

5. The earliest era is called _____.
   a. Cambrian
   b. Paleozoic
   c. Precambrian

UNIT 3 REVIEW

Circle the answer that correctly completes each of the following statements.

1. The distance in degrees east and west of the prime meridian is called _____.
   a. latitude
   b. longitude
   c. parallel

2. A problem with the Mercator projection map of the world is that _____.
   a. the map scale is too small
   b. distance is greatly distorted at high latitudes
   c. latitude and longitude are not straight parallel lines

3. Most rocks in Earth's crust are made of _____.
   a. native minerals
   b. silicate minerals
   c. nonsilicate minerals

4. When magma bulges up to make a dome, it is called a _____.
   a. sill
   b. laccolith
   c. batholith

5. A metamorphic rock made from limestone is _____.
   a. shale
   b. marble
   c. quartzite

6. In 1915, Alfred Wegener proposed a theory of _____.
   a. plate tectonics
   b. continental drift
   c. seafloor spreading

7. A volcano in the middle of a plate would have to be in a _____.
   a. hot spot
   b. rift zone
   c. subduction zone

8. An explosive volcanic eruption generally occurs in _____.
   a. a gently sloping cinder cone
   b. a gently sloping shield cone
   c. a steeply sloping composite cone

9. An imprint of a leaf is _____.
   a. a cast fossil
   b. a trace fossil
   c. not a fossil because it is not an animal

10. After 5700 years, one half of the carbon-14 in a sample has decayed.
    Over the next 5700 years, how much will decay?
    a. one quarter of the remaining carbon-14
    b. one half of the remaining carbon-14
    c. all of the remaining carbon-14

UNIT 3 APPLICATION ACTIVITY 1
Fired Up

Earth's crust moves up and down as the downward pull of the crust
interacts with the upward push of the mantle. You will see how these forces
are balanced by watching how a change in the matter of an object affects
its ability to float.

Slowly push a common pin into the bottom of a birthday candle until
the head of the pin is approximately 2 mm from the bottom of the candle.
Fill a 10-ounce glass full of water. Holding the candle by the wick, place the
candle in the water so that it floats
upright. Mark a line on the glass to
indicate the position of the bottom
of the candle.

Pin   Candle

Use a long fireplace match, or attach a clothespin to the end of a regular match. (This is so you will not burn your fingers!) Light the candle with the match, and extinguish the match. Every two minutes, mark a line on the side of the glass to indicate the position of the bottom of the candle.

1. What happened to the position of the bottom of the candle?

_____

2. As the candle melts, what happens to its weight?

_____

3. What is the relationship between weight and how high the candle floats?

_____

_____

4. How does this model relate to changes in Earth's crust and mantle?

_____

_____

_____

UNIT 3 APPLICATION ACTIVITY 2
Thar She Blows

Many landmasses—such as the Hawaiian Islands and the Galápagos Islands—were formed by volcanoes. Volcanic eruptions, such as those on Mt. St. Helens in Washington state, or on Mt. Etna in Italy, change the surface of Earth. Here you will create your own model of volcanic activity.

Put a funnel in the mouth of a 12-ounce plastic juice bottle, and pour baking soda into the bottle until it is half-full. Remove the funnel. Place the bottle in the middle of a 9-inch × 13-inch disposable aluminum baking pan. Mound moist soil around the bottle, up to its mouth. Leave the opening uncovered and free from soil.

Fill a 6- or 8-ounce cup with vinegar. Add two to three drops of red food coloring to the vinegar. Mix well.

Put the funnel back in the mouth of the bottle, and pour in the red vinegar from the cup into the bottle. Immediately remove the funnel, and stand back to watch.

1. What happens?

_____

_____

2. How does this compare to what happens in a real volcano?

_____

_____

_____

_____

UNIT 3 APPLICATION ACTIVITY 3
My Sediments Exactly

Sedimentary rocks are formed in many ways. Relatively soft compared to other types of rock on Earth, sedimentary rocks can contain fossils and can reveal information about the history of Earth and the life it supported long ago. In this activity, you will make a model that illustrates how mineral deposits cement sediments together to form a type of sedimentary rock known as sandstone.

Obtain 25 grams of alum from your instructor. Pour 100 ml of warm water into a 250-ml glass beaker. Using a stirring rod, dissolve the alum in the warm water.

Cover the bottom of a 32-ounce plastic container (such as a 2-pound margarine tub) with sand. Pour the alum solution into the container, and stir until the alum solution and sand are evenly mixed. Pour off and discard any liquid that comes to the top of the mixture. Tap the container to help the sand settle. Place the container in a safe place for 24 hours. After 24 hours, gently remove the contents.

1. Describe your rock's color, density, and overall appearance.

   _____

   _____

   _____

2. Compare your sedimentary rock to real sandstone, provided by your instructor. How is your sedimentary rock similar to sandstone?

   _____

   _____

   _____

3. How is your rock different from sandstone?

   _____

   _____

   _____

UNIT 4

Earth's Water Systems

LESSON 13: The Role of Water

GOAL: To understand the role that water plays in shaping planet Earth

WORDS TO KNOW

acid rain	deposition	rivers
atom	groundwater	runoff
bond	hydrologic cycle	soil
carbonic acid	hydrosphere	streams
chemical weathering	mechanical weathering	sublimation
compound	molecules	transpiration

The Hydrosphere

One of the things that makes Earth a unique planet in the solar system is the fact that it has liquid water on its surface. The other planets in the solar system are too hot or too cold for water to remain as a liquid. Life on Earth is dependent on water. The very first forms of life are thought to have evolved within the waters of Earth's oceans billions of years ago. When and how did Earth get its water supply? The answer lies in the origins of Earth itself.

Scientists believe that water was part of the original matter that came together to form Earth 4.6 billion years ago. The water, then in the form of water vapor, was trapped along with other gases inside the young Earth. Within the first billion years of Earth's life, volcanic outgassing released the trapped gases. Eventually, Earth cooled, the water vapor condensed, and liquid water filled the ocean basins for the first time. The water that was originally part of Earth when it formed is the same water that is here today.

You have already learned about the atmosphere around us, and the lithosphere beneath us. The other "sphere" that surrounds Earth is called the hydrosphere. The **hydrosphere** refers to all the water in the atmosphere, on Earth's surface, and within Earth's crust. If you were to take an inventory of the water in the hydrosphere, you would probably include the oceans, lakes, and rivers. Perhaps you would think of water pumped out of the ground by wells. Each of these things contains a portion of the total water on Earth's surface. It is unlikely that you would include yourself in your inventory. However, your body is almost 70% water—only a tiny part of Earth's total supply. The table below lists each of the ways that water can be stored on Earth.

Water in the Hydrosphere	
Oceans	97.2%
Glaciers	2.0%
Underground	0.5%
Surface	0.2%
Soil Moisture	0.09985%
Atmospheric moisture	0.0001%
Biological (stored in living things)	0.00005%

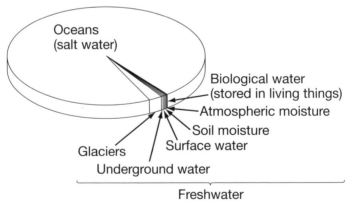

Water in the Hydrosphere

TIP

The prefix *hydr(o)*—as used in the word *hydro*sphere—means "water." Another more familiar word that uses *hydr-* is *hydr*ant (as in fire hydrant).

As you can see from the table, 97% of the water in the hydrosphere is the salty water of the oceans. The remaining 3% of the hydrosphere is freshwater. Glaciers, including the ice sheets that cover Antarctica and Greenland, make up 2% of the water. The remaining 1% of the hydrosphere is divided between underground water, surface water, moisture in the atmosphere and soil, and water stored in living things.

■ PRACTICE 47: The Hydrosphere

Decide if each statement that follows is true (**T**) or false (**F**). Write the correct letter on each line.

_____ **1.** Earth is the only planet with water in any form.

_____ **2.** The waters on Earth today have always been here.

_____ **3.** The hydrosphere only refers to all water within Earth's crust.

_____ **4.** Ocean water makes up less than half of the hydrosphere.

_____ **5.** Most of Earth's freshwater is found in glaciers.

_____ **6.** There is more water found underground than on Earth's surface.

What Is Water?

Water is the only form of matter on Earth that appears naturally not only in liquid form, but as a solid (ice), and a gas (water vapor). In the atmosphere, water changes easily and often between all three forms, as you learned in Unit 2. Water in liquid form covers most of Earth's surface, while solid water covers both poles and many mountains.

Water is made up of the elements hydrogen and oxygen. Water is not an element, but a compound. A **compound** is any substance made up of two or more elements. The smallest particle of an element is called an **atom.** Atoms combine to make **molecules.** When one atom of oxygen joins with two atoms of hydrogen, a

Water Molecule

water molecule is created. A water molecule remains the same no matter what form the water is in.

The difference between a solid, a liquid, and a gas is in how the molecules join, or **bond,** together. These differences are shown in the diagram below. Solid water, or ice, is made of water molecules bonded together in a rigid, orderly, six-sided structure. When heat energy is added and absorbed by the ice, the bonds break and the molecules can move about, sliding past one another, but staying in close contact. The ice has melted, and the water molecules are now in the form of liquid water. When more heat energy is added, the water molecules have enough energy to completely separate from one another. The water has evaporated. This means that the water molecules are now in the form of water vapor.

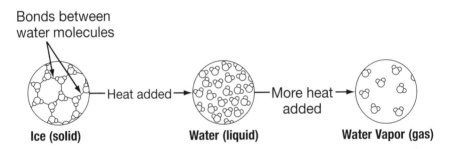

Bonds between water molecules

Heat added → More heat added →

Ice (solid)   Water (liquid)   Water Vapor (gas)

IN REAL LIFE

If you live in a part of the country where snow falls, you may have been lucky enough to observe snowflakes up close. If so, did you notice that each snowflake has a six-pointed pattern? The six points of a snowflake are a direct result of the pattern water molecules take on when they freeze.

When water cools off, the process is reversed. As energy is removed from water vapor, the water condenses, and the water molecules come together to form a liquid. As more energy is removed, the liquid water freezes, binding the molecules together in a rigid pattern.

Sometimes when ice absorbs heat energy, it changes directly to water vapor without first becoming a liquid. **Sublimation** is the term used when ice changes directly into water vapor. **Deposition** is used to describe the opposite process, when water vapor loses heat energy and changes directly to ice. Both sublimation and deposition occur in polar regions, where temperatures are always well below the freezing temperature of water, 0°C.

Most substances are the most dense in their solid form. This is not true of water. Ice is less dense than liquid water. As a result, ice floats on the water's surface. This unusual property makes it possible for life to exist in lakes and oceans even in the coldest climates. Like many substances, when water gets cooler, it becomes more dense. The loss of heat energy slows down the water molecules, bringing them closer together. Water is at its most dense just before it freezes, when the temperature reaches 4°C. When water freezes, it expands, leaving more space between the molecules, making solid water less dense than liquid water.

THINK ABOUT IT

Why is it a bad idea to put a sealed container of water or other liquid beverage into the freezer? Write your answer on a separate sheet of paper.

In a lake, the densest water sinks to the bottom. As it grows colder, and the water begins to freeze, it floats on the surface. The surface layer of ice is like a layer of insulation over the lake. It protects the pond from freezing solid. If ice were more dense than liquid water, it would sink to the bottom. Eventually, the entire lake would freeze, killing the plant and animal life in the lake.

■ PRACTICE 48: What Is Water?

Decide if each statement that follows is true (**T**) or false (**F**). Write the correct letter on each line.

_____ **1.** A water molecule is made of two atoms of oxygen and one atom of hydrogen.

_____ **2.** Water molecules are the same in solid, liquid, and gas forms.

_____ **3.** When heat is added to ice, bonds between molecules break.

_____ **4.** Water expands when it freezes.

_____ **5.** Sublimation is the term used when ice changes directly to water vapor.

_____ **6.** Water is most dense at 0°C.

_____ **7.** A surface layer of ice in a lake protects the plant and animal life within.

Weathering and Erosion

Water is needed to survive on Earth. In large amounts, such as oceans, it moderates climate. In the air, it brings rain to the dry land, replenishing wells and allowing crops to grow. In almost every way, water has a positive role. However, there is one way that water can be destructive. Water is one of the chief agents of weathering and erosion. Remember, weathering is the breaking apart of rocks due to rain, wind, freezing, and thawing. Erosion is the removal of the products of weathering by any natural agent. Natural agents of erosion are rain, wind, streams, waves, glaciers, and ocean currents. While forces within Earth create mountains, weathering and erosion destroy them.

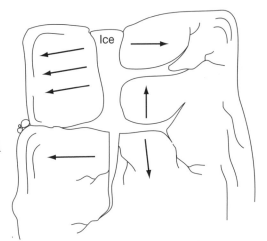

Rocks weather and crack when ice expands.

Weathering

There are two types of weathering: mechanical and chemical. **Mechanical weathering** occurs when bits of rock split and break apart into smaller pieces. The rock stays the same; only its size has changed. Water that seeps into cracks in a rock will expand when the water freezes, pushing the crack apart even more. See the illustration above. In pavement, small cracks can quickly grow into potholes.

Mechanical weathering can also occur as rocks get wet and dry over and over again. Some rocks, such as shale, will expand as water seeps in between the tiny grains. The constant swelling and shrinking will make the shale break apart.

Chemical weathering occurs when the minerals in a material react with water, water vapor, or oxygen and change into a new material. An example of chemical weathering is iron reacting with water and oxygen to form rust. Chemical weathering can also result from acid rain. **Acid rain** forms when rainwater mixes with pollutants emitted from the burning of fossil fuels. Some of the rainwater changes into nitric acid or sulfuric acid. Both of these are acidic enough to dissolve minerals in rocks. Some monuments and statues have weathered so severely due to acid rain that many of the original features are lost.

IN REAL LIFE

You have probably had firsthand experience with chemical weathering. When a car or a bike gets a scratch, it does not take long for chemical weathering to attack the metal, changing it to rust. The sooner you can protect the metal with a coat of paint, the less weathering will occur.

Normal rainwater is slightly acidic because the water mixes with carbon dioxide in the air. The resulting **carbonic acid** weathers some minerals. Carbonic acid can completely dissolve calcite, the main ingredient of limestone. Huge underground caves have been carved out of limestone by the acidic water flowing underground. You will learn more about limestone caves in Lesson 16, page 201.

One of the products of both mechanical and chemical weathering is the layer of soil that rests on top of the bedrock of the crust. **Soil** is a mixture of weathered rock and organic material. It contains minerals and nutrients that feed plants, trees, and crops. Soil is essential to life on land because it supports plant life. And, plant life is essential to protect soil from erosion. Roots of trees, shrubs, and grasses hold the soil in place. Agents of erosion are constantly removing soil. Rainwater draining into streams carries loose bits of rock and soil with it. Glaciers carry all sizes of rocks far from their source. Ocean waves and currents move sand and rocks to continually reshape the seashore.

■ PRACTICE 49: Weathering and Erosion

Decide if each of the following is a result of erosion (**E**), mechanical weathering (**M**), or chemical weathering (**C**). Write the correct letter on the line before each statement.

_____ **1.** A stream carries bits of rock downstream.

_____ **2.** Acid rain dissolves minerals in a statue.

_____ **3.** Water seeps between cracks in a rock and freezes.

_____ **4.** Ocean currents reshape a coastline.

The Water Cycle

You have already learned that the water that was part of Earth when it formed is the same water that is here on Earth today. This water has cycled through the hydrosphere over and over again. The cycle, known as the **hydrologic cycle,** or the water cycle, is driven by energy from the Sun. See the diagram below. Because of solar energy, liquid water evaporates from Earth's oceans at a rate of 129,000 cubic kilometers each year. Water vapor can also enter the atmosphere through transpiration. **Transpiration**

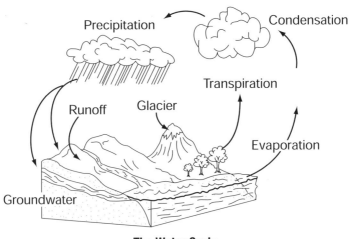

The Water Cycle

occurs when water vapor is released into the air by the leaves of plants. Winds, also driven by the Sun, carry the water vapor through the atmosphere and deposit it as rain or snow on land. Then it is gravity's turn to work on the water. The water travels downhill as **runoff,** or water that rolls off the surface without soaking into the ground. It flows into **streams** and **rivers,** or moving bodies of surface water, eventually collecting in ponds, lakes, or, ultimately, back into the oceans.

Sometimes, water temporarily leaves the water cycle. This is what happens to water trapped underground or within glaciers. When rainwater seeps into the ground, it joins the underground water supply, known as **groundwater.** Water can remain underground for thousands of years before joining surface waters through springs or wells. If precipitation falls in polar or mountainous regions, the snow may become part of a glacier and remain locked away for hundreds of years. You are also part of the water cycle. As you learned on page 162, Earth's waters cycle through you and other living creatures.

If rain comes from the oceans, why is rainwater not salty? The answer is that the salt in salt water is left behind when the water evaporates. Freshwater molecules separate from the salty ocean water to become water vapor. When water vapor condenses and falls as rain, freshwater is delivered to the land and oceans. Your body cannot survive on salt water. You need the freshwater supplied by evaporation and condensation.

THINK ABOUT IT

With all of the water evaporating out of the ocean, why does ocean water not become saltier? Write your answer on a separate sheet of paper.

■ PRACTICE 50: The Water Cycle

Circle the answer that correctly completes each of the following statements.

1. The water cycle is _____.
   a. also known as the hydrologic cycle
   b. driven by energy from the Sun
   c. different from the hydrologic cycle
   d. both *a* and *b*

2. Water vapor enters the atmosphere through _____.
    a. evaporation and transpiration
    b. condensation
    c. clouds
    d. both *a* and *b*

3. Water deposited on land as rain or snow travels downhill and collects in _____.
    a. lakes
    b. ponds
    c. oceans
    d. all of the above

4. Water can temporarily leave the water cycle through _____.
    a. glaciers
    b. rivers
    c. clouds
    d. rain

5. A _____ is NOT part of the water cycle.
    a. tree
    b. person
    c. rainstorm
    d. rock

6. It is true that _____.
    a. rainwater is salty
    b. our bodies can survive on salt water
    c. freshwater molecules separate from the ocean water to become water vapor
    d. ocean water gets saltier each time it rains

LESSON 14: Ocean Water

 GOAL: To understand the behavior of ocean water and the structure of the seafloor

WORDS TO KNOW

abyssal hills	gulfs	seas
abyssal plains	guyots	submarine canyons
atolls	gyres	surface current
bays	mixed layer	thermocline
breakers	ocean current	trough
continental margin	ocean ridges	turbidity currents
continental rise	ocean trenches	upwelling
continental shelf	oceans	vertical currents
continental slope	salinity	warm water vents
crest	sea ice	wave height
deep water	seamounts	wavelength

Oceans

Although all ocean water is connected, there are four recognized **oceans:** the Pacific Ocean, the Atlantic Ocean, the Indian Ocean, and the Arctic Ocean. Their borders are not well-defined but blend into one another. Smaller bodies of water called **seas, gulfs,** and **bays** are considered part of the larger ocean, but are surrounded on most sides by land. For example, the Gulf of Mexico, surrounded by the southern states of Florida, Alabama, Mississippi, Louisiana, and Texas on one side and the country of Mexico on the other, is considered part of the Atlantic Ocean. There is no difference between a sea, a gulf, and a bay.

The Pacific Ocean is twice as large as the Atlantic Ocean and occupies about 33% of Earth's surface—more than all the landmasses combined. Its ocean basin is slowly getting smaller as its northern and western edges are destroyed through subduction (a process by which the ocean crust plunges under the continent). Meanwhile, seafloor spreading along the Mid-Atlantic ridge keeps the Atlantic Ocean growing about 2.5 cm wider each year.

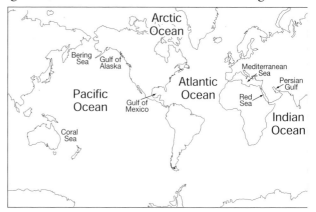

Ocean	Area (sq. km)	Average Depth (m)
Pacific Ocean	103,000,000	4030
Atlantic Ocean	51,200,000	3930
Indian Ocean	40,700,000	3960
Arctic Ocean	8,800,000	1200

Ocean water gets its saltiness from solids dissolved in it. It tastes salty because the main ingredient in ocean water is common salt, or sodium chloride. Ocean water contains other solids that are called "salts," such as magnesium chloride and calcium sulfate. If you were to take 1000 grams of seawater and let it evaporate, you would be left with about 35 grams of salt. **Salinity** is the measure of the dissolved solids in water. The salinity of ocean water averages about 35 parts of salt per 1000 parts of seawater. Ocean water has an average salinity of 35 parts per thousand.

Average salinity varies depending on the climate and location of the water. Where freshwater meets the ocean, the salinity is lower. For example, the Baltic Sea, which is located north of Europe, has a lower-than-average salinity of 30 parts per thousand. Meltwater from glaciers and runoff from streams and rivers continually dilute the salt water in the

Baltic Sea. On the other hand, if the climate near a sea or a bay is dry, the water may have a higher salinity due to evaporation. For example, the Red Sea, which is located between Africa and Saudi Arabia, has an extremely high salinity of over 38 parts per thousand. Not only is the Red Sea in a dry climate, but it has only a narrow opening to the Indian Ocean so that water cannot circulate freely.

When ocean water freezes, it is called **sea ice.** Sea ice is found throughout the year around Antarctica, within the Arctic Ocean, and in parts of the northern Atlantic Ocean. Salt water has a lower freezing temperature (–2°C) than freshwater (0°C). Thus, sea ice does not form as easily as ice on freshwater. When salt water does freeze, the salts dissolved in the water are left behind. Sea ice is made of freshwater, but the surrounding water becomes saltier in the process.

THINK ABOUT IT

How is freezing salt water similar to evaporation? Write your answer on a separate sheet of paper.

Ocean Layers

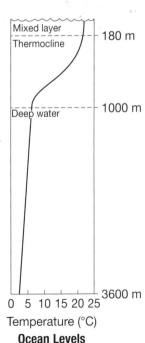

Ocean Levels

The upper 180 meters of the ocean is called the **mixed layer** because winds and waves mix the Sun's energy throughout. See the illustration on the right. Sunlight streams into this layer and provides the energy that oceans' algae need to grow. Most animal life is found in this thin, warm layer because it provides plenty of food. Temperatures are the same throughout the mixed layer, but change with latitude and with the seasons.

Between a depth of 180 meters and 1000 meters, light fades and temperatures drop rapidly. Because of the rapid change in temperature, this layer is called the **thermocline.** The lower part of this layer is completely dark, with water temperatures about 5°C for all latitudes and seasons. Despite the cold, dark water, animal life thrives in this layer. The animals feed on dead plants, on animals that fall from above, and on one another.

Most ocean water that lies beneath a depth of 1000 meters is considered deep water. **Deep water** is dark and cold, ranging from 5°C to 2°C at the ocean bottom. Changes in seasons and time of day have absolutely no effect on deep water. Food is scarce at these depths, yet some animal life exists. Around mid-ocean ridges, **warm water vents** provide enough nutrients to support a large population of animal life.

■ PRACTICE 51: Oceans

Decide if each statement that follows is true (**T**) or false (**F**). Write the correct letter on each line.

_____ **1.** The largest ocean is also the deepest ocean.

_____ **2.** Seas are larger than gulfs or bays.

_____ **3.** The main dissolved compound in ocean water is sodium chloride.

_____ **4.** The average salinity of ocean water is 35 parts of salt per 1000 parts of seawater.

_____ **5.** Ocean water freezes at a warmer temperature than freshwater.

_____ **6.** In the thermocline, temperatures drop with ocean depth.

_____ **7.** The greatest amount of ocean water lies in the mixed layer.

_____ **8.** Warm water vents are part of the layer of deep water.

Ocean Depths

The ocean floor begins where the continent ends—at the seashore. Surrounding each continent is the **continental margin,** made up of sediments eroded from the continent. These sediments are carried into the ocean by rivers or waves and deposited at varying distances from shore. The shallowest part of the continental margin, the part closest to shore, is called the **continental shelf.** Continental shelves can be anywhere from

8 kilometers to 1600 kilometers wide. Where rivers empty sediments into the sea—such as along the east coast of the United States—the continental shelf is wide. Along subduction zones, where an ocean plate

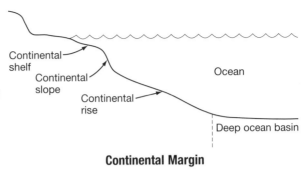

Continental Margin

sinks beneath a continental plate—such as along the west coast of South America—the continental shelf is narrow.

At the outer edge of the continental shelf, ocean depth averages about 120 meters. Here, the steep **continental slope** begins, and the ocean floor drops rapidly at a rate of 15 meters per kilometer. The entire slope is only about 200 kilometers wide. The face of the continental slope is not smooth. Instead, it has wide gullies cutting through it. The widest gullies are called **submarine canyons** and can be as wide as the Grand Canyon in Arizona. Submarine canyons are thought to have been formed by undersea landslides called **turbidity currents.** Turbidity currents can be started by a major disruption, such as an earthquake, or simply by the process of gravity. At the bottom of the continental slope is a region called the **continental rise.** The continental rise is made of sediments deposited by turbidity currents.

TIP

From its name, you might think that the continental shelf is level. But it actually has a slight slope that drops at an average rate of about 2 meters every kilometer from shore.

Deep Ocean Basins

Beyond the edge of the continental margin lie the deep ocean basins. The largest feature of the ocean basins are the vast underwater mountain ranges known as **ocean ridges.** Ocean ridges rise about 3 kilometers above the basin floor and can be 1600 kilometers wide. The Mid-Atlantic Ridge, which runs the length of the Atlantic Ocean, is part of a nearly continuous ridge system that crosses into the Indian and Pacific oceans. The entire ridge system, shown in the diagram on the right, is about 80,000 kilometers long. Ocean ridges occur at rift zones where the lithospheric plates are

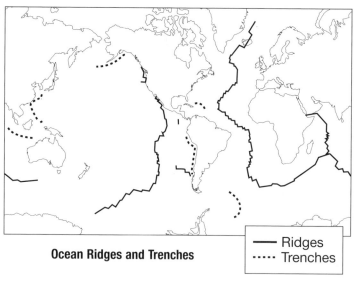

Ocean Ridges and Trenches

—— Ridges
····· Trenches

moving apart. Magma rises out of the rift, creating new seafloor that builds up to form the ridges.

Ocean trenches are the deepest part of the ocean basins. See the diagram above. While new seafloor forms at ocean ridges, old seafloor disappears into long, narrow ocean trenches. Ocean trenches occur along subduction zones where one lithospheric plate sinks beneath another. The Pacific Ocean is almost completely surrounded by ocean trenches. The longest one is the Peru-Chile trench that stretches about 8000 kilometers along the coast of South America.

Starting at the continental rise and stretching across to the ocean ridges are the abyssal plains. **Abyssal plains,** flatter and smoother than any flat plain on land, are covered with sediments from the continents that are almost a kilometer thick. Beneath the sediments are entire mountains made of volcanic rock. The mountains are the older parts of the mid-ocean ridge and have since moved far away from the rifts that created them. Some of the mountains are not entirely buried and stick up above the abyssal plain. These mountains are called **abyssal hills.**

The ocean basins also have tall volcanic mountains called **seamounts.** Sometimes the seamounts are so high that they break above the surface of the ocean and become islands. Some seamounts, called **guyots,** are flat on top. The tops were flattened by waves when the seamounts poked above the ocean surface. **Atolls** are ring-shaped islands made of tiny sea animals called coral. The coral grew around a volcanic island that has since sunk into the sea. New coral grows on top of the old coral to maintain the level of the atoll.

■ PRACTICE 52: Ocean Depths

Match each description in Column A with the correct term in Column B. Write the correct letter on each line.

Column A

_____ 1. shallowest part of the continental margin, which is also closest to the shore

_____ 2. underwater mountain range

_____ 3. gullies in the continental shelf

_____ 4. steepest part of continental margin

_____ 5. part of the continental shelf that rises from the ocean floor

_____ 6. deepest part of ocean basin

_____ 7. tall, volcanic mountains that can become islands

_____ 8. undersea landslides that can result from earthquakes

_____ 9. ring-shaped islands

_____ 10. flat-topped seamounts

_____ 11. flattest part of ocean floor

_____ 12. mountains, made of volcanic rock, mostly buried in sediments

Column B

a. abyssal plain

b. seamounts

c. continental slope

d. turbidity currents

e. guyots

f. continental rise

g. abyssal hills

h. atolls

i. ocean trenches

j. continental shelf

k. submarine canyons

l. ocean ridge

Ocean Currents

Have you ever heard of the Gulf Stream? The Gulf Stream is not really a stream, but an ocean current that flows through the North Atlantic Ocean. An **ocean current** is a wide area of ocean water that flows continually. In many ways, ocean currents are like streams. They carry water along a path from one place to another. The Gulf Stream is an example of a **surface current** because it flows horizontally across the ocean's surface. Some ocean currents are **vertical currents** that flow up and down between the ocean depths and the surface. Ocean currents continually circulate the waters of the four oceans.

Surface currents are created by the prevailing winds. When winds blow over the water's surface, they push the surface waters slowly along. However, the currents do not flow in the exact direction of the winds. The exact direction of the currents is affected by two things. First, the shape and positions of landmasses can redirect the flow of a current. Second, the Coriolis effect deflects the currents to the right or left. Remember that the Coriolis effect is a result of Earth's rotation and deflects the prevailing winds. The combination of the prevailing winds, the Coriolis effect, and landmasses creates circular currents in the open ocean called **gyres.**

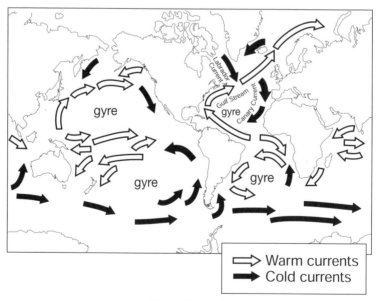

Ocean Currents

In the North Atlantic Ocean, a gyre is created by two warm-water currents on one side—the Gulf Stream and North Equatorial Current—and the Canary Current, a cold-water current, on the other. Warm water is carried away from the equator on the western side of the ocean basin. Cool water is carried away from the Pole on the eastern side of the ocean basin. Other gyres can be found in the South Atlantic, North Pacific, and South Pacific, as shown on the map on page 178.

Surface currents, such as the Gulf Stream, affect the climate of nearby landmasses. For example, the waters of the Gulf Stream are warm enough when they cross the North Atlantic that they give a temperate climate to England and parts of Norway. At the same latitude across the Atlantic, the Labrador Current, a cold-water current, gives Labrador a polar climate. The Labrador Current is responsible for carrying the fateful iceberg far enough south to be in the path of the *Titanic*.

Vertical ocean currents arise from differences in density of surface level waters. The density of ocean water is affected by the temperature and salinity of the water. Colder water and water with high salinity have the highest density. Evaporation, cooling, and freezing are all ways that water density can be affected. For example, when ocean water freezes in polar regions, the salinity of the surrounding water increases. This cold, salty water sinks to the ocean bottom and slowly travels away from the poles. The coldest, densest water in the ocean is found around Antarctica and beneath the Arctic Ocean.

Some vertical ocean currents can arise from the wind-created surface currents. Ocean water moves upward toward the surface to replace the water carried away by the surface current. Such an upward flow of ocean water is called an **upwelling.** Upwellings bring cooler water that is often rich in nutrients to the surface. Upwellings supply food for many sea animals.

Coastal weather is affected by upwellings as well. The coastal upwelling off the coast of Peru keeps the air cooler and drier than it would be if the ocean water was warmer. Every few years, however, the prevailing easterly trade winds do not blow as strongly. The surface current that normally moves toward the west reverses itself and moves toward Peru. Instead of an upwelling of cold water off the coast of Peru, there is warmer-than-normal ocean water. This warming of ocean waters is called El Niño.

During El Niño years, the normally clear, dry weather along the coast of Peru and nearby Ecuador is replaced by torrential rains that cause flooding and deadly mudslides. It is not just South American countries that are affected by El Niño. On the other side of the Pacific, cool water replaces the expected warm ocean current. Instead of rain, Indonesian countries experience a drought. The United States is also affected by El Niño. It brings sweeping rains and stormy weather to dry areas and leaves other areas drier than normal.

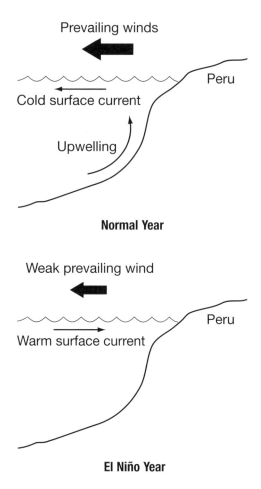

Prevailing winds

Peru

Cold surface current

Upwelling

Normal Year

Weak prevailing wind

Peru

Warm surface current

El Niño Year

IN REAL LIFE

The opposite of El Niño is La Niña, which is an event that brings unusually cool ocean temperatures to the Pacific. It has the opposite effect of El Niño on climate in North America and South America. During La Niña, weather in the Pacific Northwest is unusually wet, while weather in the Southwest and Southeast is unusually dry.

■ PRACTICE 53: Ocean Currents

Look at the list of terms below. On the line, write the letter of the term that correctly completes each statement. (*Hint:* You will not use all the terms.)

_____ 1. Currents that flow horizontally across the ocean's surface are called _____ currents.

_____ 2. Currents created by differences in water density are _____.

_____ 3. A circular current in open water is called a(n) _____.

_____ 4. _____ supply nutrients to sea animals.

_____ 5. _____ is the warming of ocean water off the coast of Peru.

_____ 6. The Canary Current is an example of a(n) _____ current.

_____ 7. Surface currents and upwellings can affect _____.

a. gyre

b. cold-water

c. upwellings

d. warm

e. surface

f. climate

g. vertical

h. El Niño

Ocean Waves

While at the seashore or on a boat in the ocean, you may have noticed that waves constantly move across the ocean's surface. Ocean waves get their start from storm winds. Tiny ripples grow into bigger waves as the wind continues to push against them. The stronger the wind and the longer it blows, the larger the waves that are generated. A hurricane covering an area of 160 kilometers with winds over 119 kilometers per hour can create waves that are 18 meters high.

The highest point of a wave is called the **crest.** The low point between crests is called the **trough. Wave height** is measured between the crest and trough as shown on the diagram on the right. **Wavelength** is the distance between crests. Generally, the wavelength is about 25 times greater than the height of the wave.

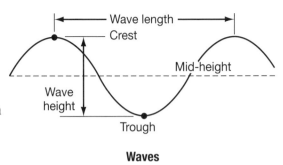

Waves

When a wave passes beneath a boat, the boat bobs up and down and rocks back and forth. However, the boat is not carried along in the direction of the wave's travel. This is because water does not travel with the wave. Instead, each point on the water's surface moves in a small circle. The bobbing and rocking that the boat experiences is the result of this circular motion. The water beneath the surface also moves in a circular pattern, although the circles become smaller and smaller as depth increases, as you can see in the diagram below. The base of the wave is considered to be at a distance of $\frac{1}{2}$ the wavelength beneath the mid-height of the wave. The mid-height of a wave is the level of the water if it were undisturbed by a wave.

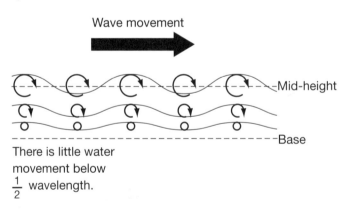

Wave movement

There is little water movement below $\frac{1}{2}$ wavelength.

If a wave does not carry water along with it, what does it carry? A wave carries energy that was transferred to the water by the wind. The wind got its energy from the Sun, as uneven heating created differences in air pressure. When you see a wave crashing on a beach, you are seeing a tiny part of the Sun's energy being released upon the shore.

Those crashing waves at the seashore are called **breakers.** When a wave moves into water shallower than $\frac{1}{2}$ a wavelength, the base of the wave drags along the sand. This dragging slows down the wave. The top of the wave, however, continues to travel toward the shore without slowing down. Eventually, the crest of the wave moves so far in front of the base that it spills forward, creating the familiar sight of crashing surf.

Not all seashores are the same. Some beaches slope steeply, while others have gentle slopes. On a steep beach, a wave can move in quite close to the shore before the base of the wave meets the ocean floor. However, when the base of the wave finally does meet the ocean floor, it slows down rapidly and the crest of the wave rises steeply. Waves on steep beaches are large and have curling tops. On a gentle beach, the base of the wave slows down gradually, farther from shore. The crest does not rise as high out of the water, making for smaller breakers.

Ocean breakers are a powerful source of erosion along coastlines. When a breaker hits a shoreline cliff, particles in the water scrape and grind the rock on the cliff. Loose bits of sand and clay are swept away from the cliff and settle along the shoreline as sediments. The sand on the beach is made from the sediments eroded from the surrounding area. Sand on a volcanic island, such as Hawaii, is made of tiny grains of basalt eroded from basalt lava that makes up most of the island.

■ PRACTICE 54: Ocean Waves

Decide if each statement that follows is true (**T**) or false (**F**). Write the correct letter on each line.

_____ **1.** A wave carries energy that was transferred to the water by the wind.

_____ **2.** Water moves in a circular pattern when a wave passes through.

_____ **3.** Wave height is measured from the midpoint to the crest.

_____ **4.** Breakers form in shallow water because the bottom half of the wave moves faster than the top.

_____ **5.** Breakers with curling tops are formed on steep beaches.

LESSON 15: Surface Water

GOAL: To understand how freshwater erodes Earth's surface

WORDS TO KNOW

advance	erratic	mountain glaciers
alluvial fans	eskers	outwash
bed	estuary	oxbow lakes
bed load	floodplain	rapids
canyons	glacier	retreat
cirque	gorges	river system
cirque horn	gullies	snout
continental glaciers	ice cave	snow line
deltas	icebergs	springs
deposition	kettle lakes	terminal moraine
divides	levees	till
drainage basin	meanders	tributaries
drift	meltwater	waterfall
drumlins	moraines	watershed

Running Water

The running water in Earth's rivers and streams would not exist without the Sun's energy. Energy from the Sun lifts millions of liters of water vapor into the air each day. When the water returns to the ground as precipitation, it can follow three different paths, each of which can become a source of a river or a stream. Rainwater that rolls off the surface without soaking into the ground is called runoff. When rainwater soaks into the ground, it joins the groundwater. Sometimes groundwater spills out of the ground in **springs.** Runoff and springs are two possible sources of a river. Another possible source of a river is **meltwater** from snow and glaciers.

All water is pulled downhill by gravity. Running water flowing from its source, usually from mountains, gathers first in gullies. **Gullies** are small valleys cut into the ground. Often gullies dry out. However, if more water pours from the source, a gully may grow larger, longer, and deeper. Remember that this process is called erosion. Eventually, the gully will be worn down so deep that it will be at the same level as the groundwater. When this happens, the gully becomes a permanent stream. The water in streams and gullies seeks the lowest point and joins together to form larger streams. The larger streams eventually empty into a river. These gullies and streams are called **tributaries** of the river because they feed into the larger river. The river and its tributaries make up the **river system.**

IN REAL LIFE

In cities and on the sides of roads, you may have seen paved gullies. These gullies are paved so that runoff will not cause further erosion.

Between the gullies and streams of a river system are highlands called **divides.** Divides separate one stream from the next. The divides and the land between them are considered the **drainage basin,** or **watershed,** of the river system. Any running water within the drainage basin will become part of the river system.

Divides also separate one watershed from another. The largest divide in the United States is the continental divide, which runs through the Rocky Mountains. A raindrop falling on the west side of the divide has fallen on either the Columbia River watershed or the Colorado River watershed. In either case, it will end up in the Pacific Ocean. Another raindrop may fall a few inches to the east in either the Mississippi River watershed or Rio Grande watershed. It will eventually make its way into the Atlantic Ocean.

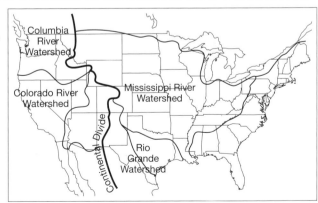

Watersheds in the United States

Running water is the strongest agent of erosion on Earth's surface. The path of a stream or river, called the **bed,** is created by erosion. Running water washes away loose soil and stones, making the streambed wider and deeper. These sediments carried by the stream are called the **bed load.** As the bed load travels along the streambed, it scrapes and scratches the bottom and sides of the bed. The streambed grows still wider and deeper. The sediments themselves are also worn down. Have you ever noticed the smooth, rounded rocks that lie on stream- and riverbeds? These river rocks have been worn down from tumbling along the bottom of the riverbed.

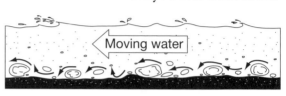

A Riverbed's Load

■ PRACTICE 55: Running Water

Match each description in Column A with the correct term in Column B. Write the correct letter on each line.

Column A

_____ **1.** stream or gully that feeds a larger river

_____ **2.** one source of a river or a stream

_____ **3.** sediments carried by stream

_____ **4.** small valleys cut into the ground

_____ **5.** highlands between streams

_____ **6.** path of stream created by erosion

_____ **7.** gully worn down to same level as groundwater

_____ **8.** divides and the land between them

_____ **9.** river and its tributaries

Column B

a. spring

b. tributary

c. divides

d. bed

e. bed load

f. watershed

g. river system

h. stream

i. gullies

The Life of a River

From its source in the mountains, running water travels through the river system toward lower ground. While still in the mountains, the river is considered a young river. When it reaches flatter land, it is a mature river, carrying a tremendous amount of water and traveling more slowly than before. The river is considered an old river as it nears the sea. Here, it slows so much that it begins to drop its load of sediments.

The Young River

The fast-moving water in a young mountain river eventually cuts a V-shaped valley into the side of the mountain. See the illustration below. If you have ever driven by or through mountains, you may have noticed these V-shaped valleys cut into the mountain slope. How do river valleys become V-shaped? If the only agent of erosion was running water in a mountain stream, the sides of the river valley would be steep. The river would cut deeper and deeper into the bottom of the bed, leaving steep valley walls. However, in most mountainous regions, rainwater is also an agent of erosion. It wears down the sides of the river valley so that the valley walls are slowly cut back. They slope gently downward like the sides of the letter V.

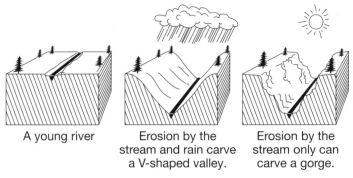

| A young river | Erosion by the stream and rain carve a V-shaped valley. | Erosion by the stream only can carve a gorge. |

River Erosion

Canyons and gorges are river valleys that have steep walls. The Grand Canyon in Colorado is a good example of a steep-walled river valley. Over the last 10 million years, spring runoff from melting snow upstream has flooded the river and cut a canyon over a kilometer deep through the Colorado Plateau. The dry climate in the region has allowed the walls of the river valley to remain steep.

Waterfalls and rapids are features of young rivers flowing through steep mountains. **Rapids** form over steeper ground and large rocks where water flows quickly enough to bubble and churn. A **waterfall** forms when the river passes from an area of hard rock to an area of softer rock. The soft rock erodes more easily than the hard rock, creating a cliff along the streambed. Water falls over the cliff, creating a waterfall. At the bottom of the waterfall, a deep pool is carved out.

The Mature River

The mature river loses some of its energy as it flows over flatter ground. As a result, it flows more slowly and begins to drop some of the larger sediments that it was carrying. **Alluvial fans** are sloping, fan-shaped deposits of sediments that form when a steep mountain stream meets drier level land. A mature river still carries silt, mud, and stones that help to grind away at the edges and bottom of the riverbed. When a mature river goes around a bend, it wears away at the bank on the outside of the bend. On the inside of the bend, the water slows down, and some of the sediments are dropped. Gradually, small bends in the river grow into larger bends called **meanders.**

The river then slowly winds its way around the meanders toward the sea. Sometimes meanders form large, U-shaped bands that get cut off from the rest of the river. These U-shaped bands eventually become small lakes called **oxbow lakes.**

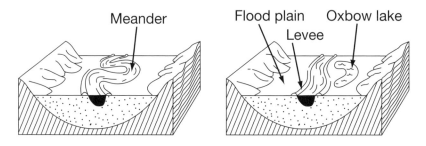

Meander   Flood plain   Oxbow lake
                        Levee

The Mature River

When the river floods and overflows its banks, it spreads out onto the surrounding **floodplain.** In some rivers, silt and mud are deposited along the banks after the flooding. These sediments build up into banks called **levees.** Levees help contain the water even when the river rises above the level of the floodplain.

The Old River

As the river gets closer to the sea, it is still carrying a tremendous amount of water, silt, and mud. It travels slowly in great meanders that become wider and wider. Instead of eating away at the sides and bottom of the riverbed, the old river now deposits its sediments. This process is called **deposition.** The river may branch into several channels separated by grassy marshes. At the mouth of many great rivers are **deltas,** fan-shaped deposits of river sediments. Deltas only form where rivers empty into protected waters without large currents and waves. As the river continues to deposit its sediments, the delta grows outward into the sea.

The Mississippi River Delta (shown on the right) in the Gulf of Mexico is formed from silt deposited from half of the continental United States. This delta has grown and changed many times over the years. In fact, much of the southern part of Louisiana was formed from Mississippi River silt deposits. These deposits have given the region rich farming soil.

When a river carries less sediment, an estuary may form instead of a delta. An **estuary** is a wide area of open water that combines freshwater from the river with salt water from the sea. Many estuaries rise and fall with the tides. The Chesapeake Bay in Maryland and Virginia is a huge estuary, home to many plants and animals.

■ PRACTICE 56: The Life of a River

Decide if each statement that follows is true (**T**) or false (**F**). Write the correct letter on each line.

_____ 1. A mature river cuts a V-shaped valley through the mountains.

_____ 2. Rapids form when young rivers flow quickly over steep land and rocks.

_____ 3. Waterfalls result when the river passes from an area of hard rock to an area of soft rock.

_____ 4. Alluvial fans can form when a steep mountain stream meets drier level land.

_____ 5. A mature river has more energy than a young river.

_____ 6. Meanders are large bends in a river.

_____ 7. Deltas can only form where rivers empty into waters without large currents and waves.

_____ 8. Oxbow lakes form along river deltas.

Glaciers

If you live in the northern part of North America, there is a good chance that the land you are standing on was once covered with glaciers. In fact, much of the landscape in your area has been shaped by glaciers. A **glacier** is a huge moving body of ice. During the peak of the last ice age—18,000 years ago—so much of the world's water supply was tied up in glacial ice that the coastlines of the continents were shifted far out to sea.

Today, glaciers remain only where the climate is cold enough year-round for snow to build up. Covering Antarctica in the south and Greenland in the north are continental glaciers. **Continental glaciers,** also called ice sheets, are large glaciers that cover almost the entire landmass. Mountain peaks poke through the continental glaciers, which can be about 3 km thick in places. When the glaciers move outward toward the seas

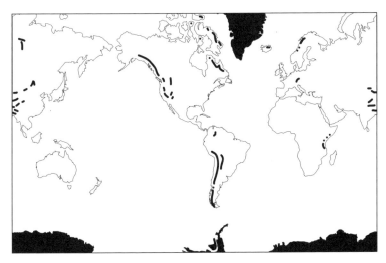

The areas in black show where glaciers are located
today. 18,000 years ago, ice covered Canada,
the northern United States, and Scandinavia.

Glaciers

under their own weight, huge chunks break off and become floating
icebergs.

Mountain glaciers, also called valley glaciers, are smaller than
continental glaciers. They lie in mountain valleys and can be hundreds of
meters thick. They form only at higher elevations and can be found even in
extremely hot areas, such as areas near the equator. The lowest elevation
where mountain glaciers can begin to form is called the **snow line.** The
snow line at the equator, where the latitude is 0°, is about 5200 meters.
At the poles, the snow line is at sea level.

How do glaciers form and of what are they made? An interesting thing
happens to snow after it falls to the ground. If you live in an area where it
snows, you may have noticed that newly fallen snow is very different from
snow that is several days old. Newly fallen snow is light and fluffy because
there are air spaces between the six-sided snow crystals. After several days,
the crystals begin to lose their shape, and the snow compresses and gets
harder. In time, the snowflakes lose their shape entirely and become hard-
packed grains of ice called firn. As more snow builds up on top, the lower
layers of firn are compressed further and changed to solid ice.

How do glaciers move? The solid ice in a glacier will flow downhill under its own weight. In Unit 3, page 109, you learned how the plastic mantle behaves due to high temperatures and pressure. In a similar way, the high pressure and effects of gravity allow glacial ice to flow downhill. Warm temperatures, a heavy snowfall, and steep slopes can all make the glacier move downhill, or **advance,** faster. If temperatures are too warm, the front of the glacier will move back, or **retreat.**

Like any solid, glacial ice can crack if it is bent too much. Crevasses are giant cracks in the glacier's surface that form when the glacier travels around a sharp bend. Another feature of a glacier is a moraine. **Moraines** are pieces of rock that fall from valley walls and are carried on the top of the glacier. Lateral moraines are long, dark lines of rocks that form on either edge of the glacier. A medial moraine runs down the middle of the glacier and forms from lateral moraines when two glaciers come together. Carried beneath the glacier are ground moraines, and at the front of the glacier is the end moraine. The end moraine is the rock pushed forward by the advancing glacier, as if by a bulldozer.

The front of the glacier is known as the **snout.** Often the opening of an ice cave is found along the base of the snout. The **ice cave** forms from glacial meltwater that pours from the opening. The meltwater is often a milky white color. Tiny, ground-up particles of rock called rock flour make a fine white sediment carried in the water. Rock flour is the result of the crushing pressure of the glacier as it scours the land beneath it.

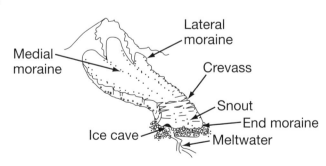

Features of a Glacier

■ PRACTICE 57: Glaciers

Circle the answer that correctly completes each of the following statements.

1. Glaciers that cover an entire landmass are called _____.
   a. valley glaciers
   b. mountain glaciers
   c. continental glaciers

2. The snow line is _____.
   a. the lowest elevation where mountain glaciers begin to form
   b. the lowest elevation where ice sheets begin to form
   c. always at sea level

3. On top of a glacier in winter, you would likely find _____.
   a. firn
   b. snow
   c. solid ice

4. Warm temperatures, heavy snow, and steep slopes will all help a glacier _____.
   a. crack
   b. retreat
   c. advance

5. Rock that falls from valley walls is called _____.
   a. firn
   b. moraine
   c. rock flour

Glaciers Carve the Land

The glaciers that once covered so much of the world have left their mark on the land. The Alps in Switzerland are an example of mountains that have been shaped by mountain glaciers. The mountain peaks are jagged and the land is rugged from the erosion caused by glaciers moving down hill. A glacier first forms high, near the mountain peak, after snow collects in a small valley. As the glacier starts to move, it scrapes at the bottom and sides of the valley. The valley gets wider and deeper. At the head of the glacier, a bowl-shaped basin called a **cirque** is carved out of the mountain. Some cirques have since filled with water and are called cirque lakes. If cirques form on all sides of a mountain peak, the peak takes on the shape of a pointy pyramid called a **cirque horn.** The Matterhorn, in the Swiss Alps, is a famous example of a horn.

You have already learned that running water in mountain streams carves V-shaped valleys in the mountain landscape. If a flowing river of glacial ice scours the river valley, it carves out a U-shaped valley. The valleys left behind after a mountain glacier has retreated have wide, flat bottoms and steep walls in the shape of a U.

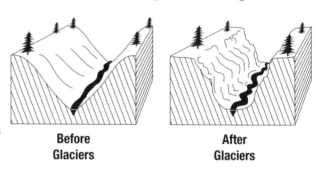

**Before
Glaciers**

**After
Glaciers**

Continental glaciers have also left their mark. The giant ice sheet that once covered Canada crept over plains and across plateaus. It completely covered the hills and many of the mountains beneath it. Instead of sharp, jagged features, continental glaciers left behind smooth round peaks.

When the last ice age ended—about 10,000 years ago—all of the rocks and debris that were carried by the glacier were left behind. Any rocky material deposited by a glacier is called **drift.** Drift can be **outwash,** deposits made by streams of meltwater, or **till,** deposits of the rocky materials carried directly by the glacier. Outwash deposits are sorted by size, since smaller particles will stay suspended in the meltwater longer. Till is unsorted and is deposited wherever the glacier left it.

Lateral and medial moraines that once lay on top of the glacier are a form of till. They become long ridges of rock that run in the same direction as the glacier. Ground moraine settles as a layer of unsorted rocks along the glacier's path. The end moraine that is left behind from the farthest advance of the glacier is called the **terminal moraine.** In some areas, there are rounded mounds of till that look like whale backs. These mounds are called **drumlins** and run in the direction of the glacier. They are believed to have been formed when a glacier ran over deposits of till left by another glacier.

Have you ever seen a huge rock perched on a hillside or in a field? The rock seems completely out of place, and it is. The rock, called an **erratic,** was left behind by a receding glacier. Often, the erratic is completely different from the rocks around it. Erratics have been found that were carried miles from their source rock.

Glacial streams running beneath the glacier deposit outwash in the ice cave. When the glacier melts, the outwash remains as long, winding ridges called **eskers.** Outwash plains are formed from rock flour, sand, and gravel that was carried beyond the terminal moraine of the glacier and deposited.

Sometimes, large chunks of ice were deposited within the drift of a glacier. When the ice melted, it left behind a depression called a kettle hole. Many kettle holes have filled with rainwater to become **kettle lakes.** Other lakes, called moraine dammed lakes, have formed when glacial moraines have been deposited in a river valley. The moraines act like a dam, blocking the flow of water and allowing a lake to fill in the valley. Sometimes the lakes that are filled in are glacial valleys, such as the Finger Lakes in New York State.

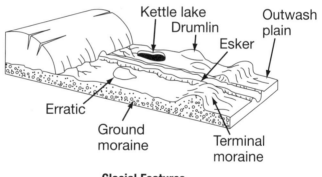

Glacial Features

The Great Lakes are also glacial lakes. Before the ice age, the area contained flat plains and several small lakes. The advancing continental glacier gouged the landscape, making the existing lakes deeper. New deep depressions were carved into the plains. When the ice sheet retreated, ice remained in the depressions. Eventually, the ice melted, forming the Great Lakes. These huge bodies of freshwater hold 40% of the fresh liquid water found on Earth's surface.

■ PRACTICE 58: Glaciers Carve the Land

Look at the list of terms below. On the line, write the letter of the term that correctly completes each statement. (*Hint:* You will not use all the terms.)

_____ **1.** A glacial valley is _____.

a. cirque horn

_____ **2.** A bowl-shaped basin at the head of a glacier is called a(n) _____.

b. drift

_____ **3.** Unsorted glacial deposits of rocky materials are called _____.

c. erratic

_____ **4.** Deposits made by streams of meltwater are called _____.

d. esker

_____ **5.** The farthest advance of a glacier is marked by the _____.

e. kettle

f. outwash

_____ **6.** A large rock left behind by a receding glacier is called a(n) _____.

g. terminal moraine

_____ **7.** A lake that lies in a hole left by a melting chunk of ice is called a(n) _____ lake.

h. till

_____ **8.** A pyramid at the top of a mountain carved by a glacier on each side of the peak is called a(n) _____.

i. U-shaped

j. cirque

_____ **9.** The _____ in Switzerland are an example of mountains shaped by glaciers.

k. drumlins

_____ **10.** Rounded mounds of till are called _____.

l. Alps

LESSON 16: Groundwater and Water Protection

 GOAL: To learn how water moves underground; to learn how to protect all of Earth's waters

WORDS TO KNOW

aquifer	groundwater	stalactites
artesian	hot springs	stalagmites
bedrock	irrigating	subsidence
cap rock	permeable	water table
eutrophication	saltwater intrusion	zone of aeration
geyser	spring	zone of saturation

Groundwater

When rainwater soaks into the ground, where does it go? It moves downward, pulled by gravity, until it reaches the huge underground supply of water known as **groundwater.** How can water move through soil? It travels through the tiny air spaces, called pore spaces, that lie between the grains of soil and rock in the ground. The amount of pore space and the rate at which the water soaks into the soil depend on the size of the grains. Coarse-grained soils like sand and gravel have large pore spaces and allow water to pass through easily. Clay is made of small, flat grains that overlap, creating small pore spaces that prevent water from passing through.

Sand, loose soil, and gravel are **permeable** materials, which means that water can flow through easily. Are rocks permeable? Some rocks are; others are not. Sandstone, which is made of grains of sand cemented together, will be permeable if there is enough space between the sand and the cement through which water can flow. Granite, however, is impermeable because the crystal grains overlap and are pressed tightly together. Shale is impermeable because its fine grains leave little pore space. However, cracks and breaks in a rock will allow water to pass through even impermeable rock.

If a soil contains both large and small grains, will it have more or less pore space than soil with just large grains? Why? Write your answer on a separate sheet of paper.

Many people who live in the country rely on wells to pump groundwater out of the ground. When the well is dug, it must reach below the top level of the groundwater. This top level is called the **water table.** The water table can vary with the season. Thus, people must dig wells deep enough to reach below the lowest level of the water table. After the spring rains, the water table is usually at its highest. The region beneath the water table is called the **zone of saturation.** The region above the water table is called the **zone of aeration.**

A person living across town from you may not need to dig as deep a well as you do in order to reach the water table. The level of the water table will depend on the topography of the area. The water table generally follows the

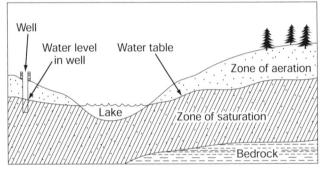

Water Table

contours of the land above. However, the water table may be farther below the surface in hilly areas than in low-lying areas. Sometimes, the water table meets the surface of the ground. On a hill, water may pour from the ground, creating a **spring.** If the ground dips down below the water table, a lake or pond will form. Year-round, streams are in low-lying areas at the level of the water table.

Groundwater is one of the main sources of drinking water for people who live in cities. When people look for groundwater, they try to find an aquifer. An **aquifer** is a layer of permeable underground rock saturated with groundwater. Groundwater flows slowly downhill through aquifers. On average, groundwater flows about 3 centimeters or less each day. Water may spend thousands of years underground before reaching the surface through a spring, stream, or lake.

TIP

The word *aquifer* comes from two Latin words that mean "to carry water."

When water from an aquifer must supply the water for an entire city, strong pumps are needed to bring the water to the surface. Once it is removed from the ground, the water is stored in huge tanks above ground until it is needed. Often, the water is filtered and treated with chlorine to kill any bacteria. The above-ground tanks supply the necessary pressure to force the water through large pipes to the residents of the city.

■ PRACTICE 59: Groundwater

Decide if each statement that follows is true (**T**) or false (**F**). Write the correct letter on each line.

_____ **1.** In general, the smaller the pore space, the more permeable the soil.

_____ **2.** If the end of a well reaches below the water table, it will be in the zone of saturation.

_____ **3.** If the ground dips below the water table, a lake will form.

_____ **4.** Water flows quickly downhill through an aquifer.

_____ **5.** When water from an aquifer must supply the water for an entire city, strong pumps are needed.

Features of Groundwater

Artesian formations are aquifers that are sandwiched between two layers of harder rock. The top layer of rock, called the **cap rock,** is impermeable and prevents rainwater from seeping through to the aquifer. The lower layer of rock, called **bedrock,** is also impermeable. Thus, water in the aquifer stays trapped between the two layers. How, then, does water enter the aquifer in the first place? Rainwater enters the aquifer uphill at a location where there is no cap rock. The collecting area for an artesian formation can be many kilometers away. In the Midwest, a sandstone aquifer, called the Dakota Sandstone, carries waters to the Great Plains. Yet, the collecting area for the aquifer is in the Rocky Mountains, hundreds of kilometers away.

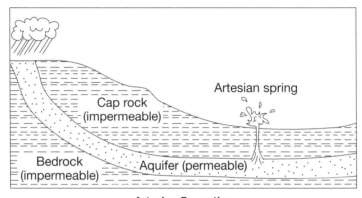

Artesian Formation

All along the aquifer, the water is under pressure from the weight of the water behind it. When wells, called artesian wells, are drilled through the cap rock, water rises on its own. No pump is needed to pull the water from the ground. Wherever cracks form in the cap rock, artesian springs gush water above the surface like a fountain.

Have you ever seen Old Faithful erupt? Old Faithful is a geyser in Yellowstone National Park. A **geyser** is a spring that shoots out heated water and steam. Every hour or so, hot water comes shooting out of the ground sending a fountain of water over 30 meters into the air. In areas of volcanic activity, groundwater may sink deep into the ground. At these areas of great depth and pressure, magma can heat the water to above its boiling point. This superheated water eventually boils and sends any water that lies above it shooting out of the ground through a narrow opening. After an eruption, new water moves in, becomes superheated, and in time erupts again from the ground. Old Faithful got its name because the time between eruptions is very regular and predictable.

Not all heated groundwater erupts. Sometimes, it pours gently from the ground in **hot springs.** Many hot springs are formed from extremely deep artesian aquifers, where the water has come in contact with heat from Earth's interior. Near areas of volcanic activity, hot springs form from shallower groundwater heated by hot igneous rocks.

All groundwater contains more minerals than rainwater because it has passed through soil and rock that contain many minerals. Hot springs often produce water rich in dissolved minerals. The hotter the water, the more minerals will dissolve. The minerals can be found along the edges of hot springs where they are deposited after the water cools.

One of the minerals that can dissolve in groundwater is calcite. Calcite is found in the sedimentary rock limestone. You learned in Unit 3 that calcite and limestone will bubble and fizz when a weak acid is dropped on them. The bubbling and fizzing is the limestone dissolving. In Lesson 13, on page 167, you also learned that carbonic acid in rainwater can produce chemical weathering of limestone. Groundwater can do even more damage, since it picks up more carbonic acid after passing through the soil. The carbonic acid slowly eats away at the limestone. Small cracks will, in time, grow into larger cracks as the acidic groundwater flows

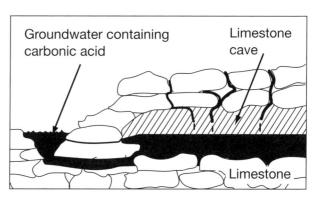

through the limestone. After many thousands of years, an underground cave or cavern forms in the limestone with a river of groundwater running through the middle of it.

Calcite deposits are found within the cavern where the groundwater evaporated. **Stalactites** made of calcite hang like icicles from the ceiling of the cave. Water leaks in through the ceiling, runs down the stalactites and drips onto the floor of the cave beneath. **Stalagmites** are upright pillars that build up under stalactites. Limestone caverns are found in New York, Kentucky, Virginia, Oregon, South Dakota, New Mexico, and many other places.

■ PRACTICE 60: Features of Groundwater

Decide if each statement that follows is true (**T**) or false (**F**). Write the correct letter on each line.

_____ **1.** The collecting area for an artesian formation is never more than a few meters away from the formation.

_____ **2.** Strong pumps are needed to remove water from an artesian well.

_____ **3.** Groundwater can be heated either by magma or by hot igneous rocks.

_____ **4.** Limestone caves are carved by groundwater that contains carbonic acid.

_____ **5.** Hot groundwater has fewer minerals than cold groundwater.

Water Overuse

Earth is called the water planet because water covers about 70% of its surface. The water on Earth is the most precious resource we have. You and most other living things need water to survive. There seems to be so much water on Earth, yet the sources of freshwater are limited. Of all of Earth's waters, 97% is salty ocean water, unfit for drinking. The remaining 3% is freshwater, but most of it is unusable, since it is either frozen in glaciers or buried too deep in the ground to be removed. Only 0.003% of all of Earth's water is available as groundwater, water in lakes and streams, or as water vapor in the atmosphere.

With so little usable water available, you can see why it is important to protect this natural and precious resource. In this country, freshwater is used in agriculture, industry, and by the general public for their personal needs. The average American uses over 400 liters a day for personal use. One of the problems facing this country and other countries around the world is the overuse of water.

As you have already learned, groundwater moves slowly through underground aquifers. If water is removed from one part of an aquifer too quickly, it can take a long time for new water to recharge it. Most aquifers are recharged naturally by rainfall. If the rate of removal is greater than the rate of recharge, problems arise that go beyond just several dry wells.

First, if any pollutants or animal waste spill onto the land above the area of the well, they will seep quickly through the soil and be pulled directly from the well. Second, the land above the aquifer can sink, or subside. The resulting land **subsidence** can lead to sink holes that damage pipelines, highways, and buildings. Finally, if the aquifer is near the ocean, salt can intrude, or move into the freshwater aquifer. **Saltwater intrusion** can contaminate the aquifer and make it unsafe to use.

Overuse of available surface water can also cause problems. In California, most of the population lives in the southern half of the state. But most of the rain occurs in the northern half of the state. To help solve this problem, water from the plentiful watersheds in the north is sent to the drier areas in the south. However, residents in the north are worried that the natural rivers in their area are losing too much water. The rivers might soon be unable to support the fish and wildlife population.

Solutions

Today, more and more efforts are being made to conserve freshwater. On farms, better ways of watering, or **irrigating,** the crops are being used. It is estimated that more than half of the water that people use is wasted through leaks in pipes, evaporation, and dripping faucets. Fixing leaky pipes and faucets, installing low-flow showerheads, and watering gardens and lawns in the morning or evening when there is less evaporation are several ways that water can be conserved.

THINK ABOUT IT

Can you think of ways that you can conserve water? Write your answer on a separate sheet of paper.

■ PRACTICE 61: Water Overuse

Decide if each statement that follows is true (**T**) or false (**F**). Write the correct letter on each line.

_____ **1.** Most of Earth's freshwater is unusable.

_____ **2.** The average American uses over 400 liters of water a day for personal use.

_____ **3.** Overuse of groundwater occurs when the rate of recharge is greater than the rate of removal.

_____ **4.** The most serious result of groundwater overuse is the dry wells.

_____ **5.** Better methods of irrigating crops will help to solve problems of water overuse.

Water Pollution

Water pollution threatens all forms of life. One hundred years ago, the most damaging source of water pollution was sewage and animal waste. Today, the industrialized world has created many other sources of pollution. Pollutants can make their way into groundwater, surface waters, and ocean water.

Pollution of Groundwater

The most common pollutants found in groundwater come from fertilizers and pesticides used in farming. These pollutants can seep directly into the ground when they are sprayed onto crops. Road salt used to melt ice poses another problem.

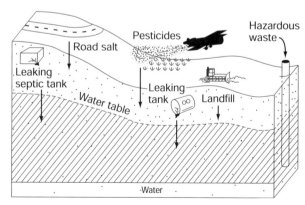

Pollution of Groundwater

Groundwater can also be polluted from leakage of underground tanks that store oil and gas. Hazardous chemicals in landfills can also seep into the groundwater. Some septic systems spill waste into the ground. Some industries inject their hazardous waste deep into the ground.

Pollution of Surface Water

Pollution of lakes and streams has been greatly reduced in the last 25 years. At one point, industries could send their waste products directly into a river. Today, many streams have been cleaned up due to environmental regulations. Because the water in a stream flows quickly and is always being replaced by new water upstream, streams clean up more easily than lakes or groundwater.

Since there is often little flow of water in a lake, it will suffer from pollutants more than a stream. One of the biggest problems is lake eutrophication. **Eutrophication** of a lake happens when too many plant nutrients enter a lake and change the balance of life in the lake. Acid rain can also affect the life of a lake.

Pollution of Ocean Water

Oceans are the final resting point of Earth's surface waters. Oceans are so large that sewage and other pollutants are greatly diluted. However, shallow coastal waters are closest to the human sources of pollution. Beaches near cities are sometimes closed because of high levels of bacteria that could make swimmers sick. The bacteria enter the water when a city's sewage system becomes overloaded. Estuaries, such as the Chesapeake Bay, have suffered in much the same way as lakes have. Water from many rivers drain into the Chesapeake, bringing in plant nutrients and other pollutants.

Oil spills can harm ocean water and the life that depends on it. Since oil floats on water, much of it can evaporate from the surface. However, some types of oil do not evaporate and instead form thick black globs that coat the feathers of birds and the fur of marine animals. Not all oil spills are from oil tanker accidents at sea. Almost half of the oil that ends up in the ocean comes from the land. Waste oil runs into the streams that ultimately empty into the oceans. When you change your car's engine oil, be sure to dispose of it properly. You never know where it will end up.

Solutions

Solutions to problems of water pollution are slow to come. Some problems require changing long-standing habits, such as the way fertilizers and pesticides are used in farming. Industries, too, face tougher laws in carrying and disposing of hazardous materials. Polluted groundwater is a more difficult problem to solve. Once groundwater is polluted, it is very difficult to clean up. Solutions are costly and impractical. The best way to control groundwater pollution is to protect the groundwater in the first place.

You can help, too. You can check your septic system and underground storage tanks for leaks. You can ask your local authorities for the best way to safely dispose of household chemicals in your city or town. Batteries, paint, and oil are considered hazardous waste and must be disposed of properly. It is important to protect Earth's limited supply of freshwater— water that has helped support life for 3.5 billion years. The water on Earth has been here for 4.6 billion years. In that time, it has cycled through the air and ground many times.

■ PRACTICE 62: Water Pollution

Decide if each of the following examples is mainly a form of groundwater pollution (**G**), surface water pollution (**S**), or ocean water pollution (**O**). Write the correct letters on each line. (*Hint:* More than one type of pollution may be used for some of the examples.)

_____ **1.** fertilizers and pesticides

_____ **2.** oil spills

_____ **3.** road salt

_____ **4.** leaking septic system

_____ **5.** eutrophication

_____ **6.** dumping of waste products

UNIT 4 REVIEW

Circle the answer that correctly completes each of the following statements.

1. The largest part of the hydrosphere is _____.
   a. glaciers
   b. oceans
   c. atmospheric moisture

2. The largest part of freshwater on Earth is _____.
   a. trapped in glaciers
   b. underground
   c. atmospheric moisture

3. When heat energy is added to ice, _____.
   a. the bonds between the hydrogen and oxygen atoms break
   b. the bonds between water molecules break
   c. the bonds between the hydrogen atoms break

4. The ocean layer with the most life in it is _____.
   a. deep water
   b. the mixed layer
   c. the thermocline

5. Ocean waves carry _____.
   a. energy
   b. water
   c. wind

6. V-shaped valleys are produced by _____.
   a. streams
   b. glaciers
   c. lack of rainfall

7. Running water flowing from its sources gathers first in _____.
   a. gullies
   b. streams
   c. divides

8. A river's drainage basin is also called a _____.
   a. delta
   b. watershed
   c. tributary

9. If a rock is permeable, it has _____.
   a. large pore spaces
   b. no cracks or breaks in it
   c. either *a* or *b*

10. When the water table meets the surface of the ground, _____.
    a. a spring may form
    b. a pond has most likely dried up
    c. the water is no longer available for use by people

UNIT 4 APPLICATION ACTIVITY 1
Water Wear

You may have seen the effects of erosion on riverbanks or gorges. Try your own demonstration to see how water erosion works.

Obtain two bars of soap that are the same size and brand. Adjust the flow of water from a faucet so that the water drips slowly and steadily. In the chart, record how many drops of water are released per minute.

	Soap 1	Soap 2
Drops per minute		
Time (begin)		
Time (end)		
Appearance		

Unwrap the two bars of soap. Put one bar directly under the dripping faucet. Place the other bar of soap in a dry place. Record the time you put the soap under the faucet and the time you placed the second soap in a dry place.

After a few hours, turn off the water. Record the appearance of each bar of soap.

1. How do the two soaps differ?

_____

2. How can you speed up the process of erosion in this experiment?

_____

3. How can you slow it down?

_____

4. What can you infer about the effect of water on stone?

_____

_____

_____

UNIT 4 APPLICATION ACTIVITY 2
Glacial Flow

In this activity, you will see how a substance such as hard, solid ice can bend and flow.

Fill a long tray (about 10 centimeters wide by 20 centimeters long) with just over a centimeter of water. Put the tray in the freezer. The next day, carefully remove the ice block from the tray.

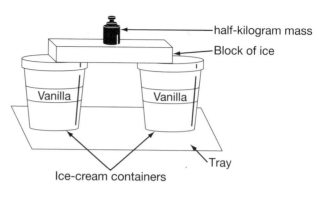

In the freezer, place two plastic objects approximately 10 centimeters tall (such as two 1-quart ice-cream containers) at each end of the tray.

Place the ice on top of the supports to make a bridge. Then place a half-kilogram mass on top of the ice.

Observe the ice every day for three days. Record your observations in the chart below.

Day	Observations
1	
2	
3	

1. What happened to the ice?

_____

2. Why did this occur?

_____

3. What causes ice to flow in a glacier?

_____

4. Would you expect a glacier in a valley to move faster on its sides or in the middle?

_____

5. What causes the downhill movement of a glacier?

_____

UNIT 4 APPLICATION ACTIVITY 3
Mystery Boulders

Sometimes boulders appear on the ocean floor where they do not seem to belong. In this activity, you will see how "out-of-place" boulders can appear far out in the ocean.

Freeze a pebble and some sand in one cube of an ice-cube tray. Float the ice cube in a pan or a glass of water.

1. What do you observe?

_____

_____

2. How do "out-of-place" boulders most likely get to their locations in the ocean?

_____

_____

_____

3. Why are these boulders called glacial deposits?

_____

_____

_____

APPENDIXES

A. Terrestrial Planets Chart

Planet	Astronomical Unit Distance (Earth is 1)	Average Distance to Sun (in kilometers)	Approximate Length of Year (Revolution Around Sun)	Approximate Length of Day (Rotation Around Axis)	Diameter (in kilometers)
Mercury	0.39	57.9 million	88 Earth days	59 Earth days	4880
Venus	0.72	108.2 million	225 Earth days	243 Earth days	12,104
Earth	1	149.6 million	365 Earth days	1 Earth day	12,756
Mars	1.52	227.9 million	687 Earth days	1 Earth day	6794
Pluto	39.48	5.9 billion	248 Earth years	6 Earth days	2302

B. Jovian Planets Chart

Planet	Astronomical Unit Distance (Earth is 1)	Average Distance to Sun (in kilometers)	Approximate Length of Year (Revolution Around Sun)	Approximate Length of Day (Rotation Around Axis)	Diameter (in kilometers)
Jupiter	5.20	778.4 million	12 Earth years	10 hours	142,984
Saturn	9.54	1.4 billion	29 Earth years	11 hours	120,536
Uranus	19.19	2.9 billion	84 Earth years	17 hours	51,118
Neptune	30.07	4.5 billion	165 Earth years	16 hours	49,528

C. Geologic Timetable

Geologic Timetable			
Era	**Era Began**	**Era Ended**	**Highlights of Era**
Cenozoic—includes the Quaternary and Tertiary periods	65 million years ago	Present day	"Age of Mammals." Many new mammals appear. Homo sapiens appear. (300,000 years ago). Modern humans become dominant during the last 11,000 years. Ice ages during the last 2 million years.
Mesozoic—includes the Cretaceous, Jurassic, and Triassic periods	250 million years ago	65 million years ago	"Age of Reptiles." Reptiles thrive. First birds and mammals appear. Dinosaurs die out by end of era. Atlantic Ocean begins to form.
Paleozoic—includes the Permian, Devonian, and Cambrian periods, among others	570 million years ago	250 million years ago	"Age of Invertebrates." First fish, amphibians, reptiles, and marine animals. Trilobites are alive during the earliest Cambrian period. Super-continent of Pangaea forms.
Precambrian	4.6 billion years ago	570 million years ago	Soft-bodied marine animals: jellyfish, worms. No life on the land. Volcanic activity produces Earth's atmosphere.

GLOSSARY

absolute age (AB-suh-loot AYJ) the actual age of a fossil, determined using radiometric dating techniques

absolute magnitude (AB-suh-loot MAG-nuh-tood) how bright a star really is, from a standard distance

abyssal hills (uh-BI-sul HILZ) hills on the ocean bottom that are not entirely covered with sediment

abyssal plains (uh-BI-sul PLAYNZ) the flat bottoms of the ocean between the continental rise and the ocean ridges

acid rain (A-sud RAYN) the mixture of rainwater with emission from fossil fuels

advance (ud-VANS) the forward growth of a glacier during the cold season

aftershocks (AF-tur-shoks) secondary earthquakes that shake the ground after the large earthquake; aftershocks can cause significant damage.

air mass (AR MAS) a large body of air that has nearly the same temperature and humidity throughout

air pressure (AR PRE-shur) the weight of air on a given area

alluvial fans (uh-LOO-vee-ul FANZ) flood plains that form when a steep mountain stream meets drier, more level land

altitude (AL-tuh-tood) the distance from sea level of a place in the atmosphere or on a mountain

aphelion (a-FEEL-yun) the position of Earth when it is farthest from the Sun

PRONUNCIATION KEY

CAPITAL LETTERS show the stressed syllables.

a	as in mat	f	as in fit
ay	as in day, say	g	as in go
ch	as in chew	i	as in sit
e	as in bed	j	as in job, gem
ee	as in even, easy, need	k	as in cool, key

apogee (A-puh-jee) the position where the Moon is farthest from Earth

apparent magnitude (uh-PAR-unt MAG-nuh-tood) how bright a star appears to be from an observer's position

aquifer (A-kwuh-fur) water-bearing underground rock

artesian (or-TEE-zhun) an aquifer that is sandwiched between two layers of harder rock

asterisms (AS-tuh-ri-zumz) partial constellations, or groupings of stars from several constellations, that form a recognizable pattern; the Big Dipper in the constellation Ursa Major is an asterism. The Summer Triangle, which contains stars from three separate constellations, is also an asterism.

asteroids (AS-tuh-roydz) small, planetlike bodies; asteroids are mainly found in the asteroid belt, which lies between Mars and Jupiter.

asthenosphere (as-THE-nuh-sfir) the lower mantle, which is plastic and moves in convection cycles

astronomy (uh-STRO-nuh-mee) the study of the universe

atolls (A-tolz) ring-shaped islands made of coral

atom (A-tum) the smallest particle of matter that maintains its own chemical characteristics

aurora (uh-ROHR-uh) an event in Earth's magnetic field in which solar wind interacts with the magnetic field and causes flickering red and green lights; auroras are most common around the North and South Poles.

barometer (buh-RO-muh-tur) an instrument for measuring air pressure

---

PRONUNCIATION KEY

CAPITAL LETTERS show the stressed syllables.

ng	as in running	u	as in but, some
o	as in cot, father	uh	as in about, taken, lemon, pencil
oh	as in go, note	ur	as in term
sh	as in shy	y	as in line, fly
th	as in thin	zh	as in vision, measure
oo	as in too		

basalt (buh-SOLT) an igneous rock formed from lava

batholith (BA-thuh-lith) a large area underground filled with cooled magma

bays (BAYZ) inlets from an ocean; bays are salt water.

bed (BED) the path of a stream or a river

bed load (BED LOHD) the amount of soil or rock a river can carry

bedrock (bed-ROK) the impermeable layer beneath the artesian formation

Big Bang (BIG BANG) the theory that the origin of the universe was an explosion of energy 12 to 15 billion years ago

binary stars (BY-nuh-ree STARZ) stars that have a system with two or more stars

black hole (BLAK HOHL) extremely dense region with gravity so strong that the escape velocity from the region is greater than the speed of light

bond (BOND) to join together, as two or more atoms join to form a molecule

breakers (BRAY-kurz) waves that reach the beach; as the ocean becomes shallow, all the energy is forced up, making breakers tall.

calcite (KAL-syt) a mineral in limestone

caldera (kal-DER-uh) a crater left over after a volcanic eruption

canyons (KAN-yunz) river valleys with steep sides; usually, canyons occur where there is little rainfall.

PRONUNCIATION KEY

CAPITAL LETTERS show the stressed syllables.

a	as in mat	f	as in fit
ay	as in day, say	g	as in go
ch	as in chew	i	as in sit
e	as in bed	j	as in job, gem
ee	as in even, easy, need	k	as in cool, key

cap rock (KAP ROK) the impermeable barrier between an artesian formation and the surface

carbon dating (KAR-bun DAY-ting) a radiometric dating technique using carbon-14, which is found in all living things

carbonic acid (kar-BO-nik A-sud) the mixture of rainwater with carbon dioxide

Cepheid variables (SE-fee-id VER-ee-uh-bulz) stars that get brighter and dimmer at regular intervals

chemical sedimentary rocks (KE-mi-kul se-duh-MEN-tuh-ree ROKS) any sedimentary rocks formed from the minerals left behind as ocean water evaporates, or when dissolved chemicals combine and become solid, such as the rock formations in caves

chemical weathering (KE-mi-kul WETH-ring) the breaking apart of rocks due to changes in the soil or acid rain

chromosphere (KROH-muh-sfir) a thin layer of gases surrounding the Sun; the chromosphere has a pinkish glow, usually invisible during the day.

cinder cone (SIN-dur KOHN) a volcano formed from ash and cinders

circumpolar (sur-kum-POH-lur) describes a constellation that seems to revolve around Polaris without setting or rising

cirque (SURK) a bowl-shaped basin carved out of a mountain by a glacier

cirque horn (SURK HORN) a mountain peak carved by glaciers in the shape of a pointy pyramid

cirrus (SIR-us) describes high, icy clouds that look wispy from the ground

---

PRONUNCIATION KEY

CAPITAL LETTERS show the stressed syllables.

ng	as in running	u	as in but, some
o	as in cot, father	uh	as in about, taken, lemon, pencil
oh	as in go, note	ur	as in term
sh	as in shy	y	as in line, fly
th	as in thin	zh	as in vision, measure
oo	as in too		

clastic (KLAS-tik) formed from sediments that have been weathered, or eroded, from other rock

cleavage (KLEE-vij) the ability of a mineral to split along flat surfaces

climate (KLY-mut) the overall average weather of a given area

coal (KOHL) a substance made from the remains of plants that were buried and compacted millions of years ago

cold front (KOHLD FRUNT) a front in which the cold air mass moves more quickly than the warm air mass

comets (KO-muts) icy, dusty rocks from far out in the solar system; comets occasionally fall toward the center of the solar system and begin to evaporate. As they do, the water vapor and dust trails are blown back by the solar wind, creating a "tail."

composite cone (kom-PO-zut KOHN) a volcano formed from lava and ash

compound (KOM-pownd) any substance made up of two or more elements

condensation (kon-den-SAY-shun) the passing of water from the gas state to the liquid state

cone (KOHN) layers of lava that build up over time to form a mountain shape

conglomerate (kun-GLOM-rut) a sedimentary rock containing large particles such as pebbles that have been naturally cemented together

constellations (kon-stuh-LAY-shunz) groupings of stars that form a recognizable pattern; there are 88 constellations.

PRONUNCIATION KEY

CAPITAL LETTERS show the stressed syllables.

a	as in mat	f	as in fit
ay	as in day, say	g	as in go
ch	as in chew	i	as in sit
e	as in bed	j	as in job, gem
ee	as in even, easy, need	k	as in cool, key

contact metamorphism (KON-takt me-tuh-MOR-fi-zum) changes that occur to rock when it comes into contact with hot magma

continental air mass (kon-tun-EN-tul AR MAS) an air mass that forms over land

continental crust (kon-tun-EN-tul KRUST) the crust below Earth's landmasses, which is thicker than the oceanic crust

continental drift (kon-tun-EN-tul DRIFT) An older theory of plate movement, this theory proposed the now widely accepted notion of the continent of Pangaea, in which all the continents were formed as one large landmass.

continental glaciers (kon-tun-EN-tul GLAY-shurz) also called ice sheets; glaciers that cover a large landmass

continental margin (kon-tun-EN-tul MAR-jun) a region surrounding the continents containing sediments that washed out to sea from continental rivers

continental rise (kon-tun-EN-tul RYZ) a region at the bottom of the continental slope, caused by a piling up of sediments

continental shelf (kon-tun-EN-tul SHELF) the shallowest part of the continental margin, closest to the shore

continental slope (kon-tun-EN-tul SLOHP) the decline from the continental shelf to the deep water

contour lines (KON-tur LYNZ) lines on a topographic map that connect points of equal elevation

---

PRONUNCIATION KEY

CAPITAL LETTERS show the stressed syllables.

ng	as in running	u	as in but, some
o	as in cot, father	uh	as in about, taken, lemon, pencil
oh	as in go, note	ur	as in term
sh	as in shy	y	as in line, fly
th	as in thin	zh	as in vision, measure
oo	as in too		

contract (kun-TRAKT) come closer together

convection cell (kun-VEK-shun SEL) the rising, moving, and sinking of an air mass

convective zone (kun-VEK-tiv ZOHN) region in the body of the Sun where energy rises and gases boil

Coriolis effect (kohr-ee-OH-lus i-FEKT) the change in the path of any object traveling above Earth's surface, caused by Earth's rotation

corona (kuh-ROH-nuh) the huge outer atmosphere of the Sun, which stretches for millions of kilometers into space

cosmologists (koz-MO-luh-jists) those who study the origins of the universe

crescent moon (KRE-sunt MOON) the phase of the Moon during which a thin sliver is lighted and visible

crest (KREST) the top of a wave

crust (KRUST) the outer skin of Earth, made of rocks, and containing all surface water sources

crystal (KRIS-tul) solid form of a substance that has a regularly repeating internal arrangement of atoms or molecules

crystalline solid (KRIS-tuh-lun SO-lud) mineral in which the atoms arrange themselves in a regular pattern

cumulonimbus (kyoo-myuh-loh-NIM-bus) describes clouds in which thunderstorms form

---

PRONUNCIATION KEY

CAPITAL LETTERS show the stressed syllables.

a	as in mat	f	as in fit
ay	as in day, say	g	as in go
ch	as in chew	i	as in sit
e	as in bed	j	as in job, gem
ee	as in even, easy, need	k	as in cool, key

cumulus (KYOO-myuh-lus) describes fair-weather, puffy clouds that form low in the sky

deep water (DEEP WO-tur) any ocean water below a depth of 1000 meters

degrees (di-GREEZ) the measure of a position on a circle; there are 360° in a circle.

deltas (DEL-tuhz) fan-shaped deposits of river sediments at the mouth of a river

deposition (de-puh-ZI-shun) the changing of a gas into a solid without moving first through the liquid state of matter; the deposit of sediments

dew (DOO) condensed water vapor, often seen on grass in the morning after a cool night

dew point (DOO POYNT) the temperature at which water vapor condenses; this varies according to the level of humidity in the atmosphere.

dike (DYK) a rock formation in which magma cuts through several layers of existing rock

divides (duh-VYDZ) highlands separating water drainage systems

doldrums (DOHL-drumz) a low pressure belt at the equator, where the winds die

dome mountains (DOHM MOWN-tunz) mountain formation in which a laccolith from underground pushes up under the crust; the ground above bulges upward, creating a mountain. The Henry Mountains in Utah are an example of dome mountains.

PRONUNCIATION KEY

CAPITAL LETTERS show the stressed syllables.

ng	as in running	u	as in but, some
o	as in cot, father	uh	as in about, taken, lemon, pencil
oh	as in go, note	ur	as in term
sh	as in shy	y	as in line, fly
th	as in thin	zh	as in vision, measure
oo	as in too		

drainage basin (DRAY-nij BAY-sun) a region connected with a particular stream or river; water that falls in the drainage basin will enter that river.

drift (DRIFT) rocky material deposited by a glacier

drumlins (DRUM-lunz) round mounds of rocky material left by a glacier

earth science (URTH SY-uns) the study of Earth and all its systems

earthquake (URTH-kwayk) shaking of the ground that follows a plate movement

eclipse (i-KLIPS) the passing of one celestial body between two others, causing one of them to dim or go dark; solar eclipses are caused by the Moon passing between Earth and the Sun. Lunar eclipses are caused by the Earth passing between the Sun and the Moon.

El Niño (el-NEE-nyoh) changes to the climate based on a periodic warming of the ocean waters off the coast of Peru

electromagnetic spectrum (i-lek-troh-mag-NE-tik SPEK-trum) the total range of all electromagnetic waves

elevation (e-luh-VAY-shun) the distance from sea level for an object above water

elliptical galaxies (i-LIP-ti-kul GA-luk-seez) galaxies without arms; elliptical galaxies are usually older galaxies.

energy budget (E-nur-jee BUH-jut) an accounting of how Earth uses the incoming solar energy

epicenter (E-pi-sen-tur) the place directly above the place where the plates that caused the earthquake moved

---

PRONUNCIATION KEY

CAPITAL LETTERS show the stressed syllables.

a	as in mat	f	as in fit
ay	as in day, say	g	as in go
ch	as in chew	i	as in sit
e	as in bed	j	as in job, gem
ee	as in even, easy, need	k	as in cool, key

epochs (E-puks) divisions of geologic time that are less than a period and greater than an age

equator (i-KWAY-tur) an imaginary line that circles Earth at the north-south center of Earth

equinoxes (EE-kwuh-nok-sez) the two days during the year when the Sun appears directly over the equator; they are the first day of spring and the first day of autumn.

eras (IR-uhz) largest divisions of time in the geologic timetable

erosion (i-ROH-zhun) the removal of the products of weathering by any natural agent

erratic (i-RA-tik) a rock left behind by a retreating glacier

eskers (ES-kurz) long, winding ridges of outwash left by a glacial stream

estuary (ES-chuh-wer-ee) a wide area of open water that combines fresh-water from a river with salt water from an ocean

eutrophication (yoo-troh-fuh-KAY-shun) condition in a lake when too many plant nutrients (usually runoff from agriculture) enter the lake and cause too many plants to grow in the lake; this often has serious consequences for the other life-forms.

evaporation (i-va-puh-RAY-shun) the passing of water from the liquid state to the gas state

expands (ik-SPANDZ) gets larger

extrusive rocks (ik-STROO-siv ROKS) magma that reaches the surface and cools on the surface, or underwater

---

PRONUNCIATION KEY

CAPITAL LETTERS show the stressed syllables.

ng	as in running	u	as in but, some
o	as in cot, father	uh	as in about, taken, lemon, pencil
oh	as in go, note	ur	as in term
sh	as in shy	y	as in line, fly
th	as in thin	zh	as in vision, measure
oo	as in too		

eye (Y) the calm center of a hurricane or tropical storm, when winds die and rain stops

fault (FOLT) any crack in the crust where there is movement

fault-block mountains (FOLT-BLOK MOWN-tunz) mountain formation in which one block of land is forced up above the other; the Sierra Nevadas are fault-block mountains.

felsic magma (FEL-sik MAG-muh) light, thick, pasty magma, high in silicate content

floodplain (FLUD-playn) a low-lying region where a river floods and overflows its banks, close to the end of the river

focus (FOH-kus) the point underground where an earthquake occurs

fog (FOG) a mass of air cooled below its dew point, leaving a cloud near the surface of Earth

fold mountains (FOHLD MOWN-tunz) mountain formation in which two plates collide, forcing up the edges of the plate; the Himalayas are fold mountains.

fossil fuels (FO-sul FYOOLZ) forms of energy, such as coal, gas, and petroleum, that have their origins in the living things of long ago

fossils (FO-sulz) any evidence of past plant or animal life found in rocks

fracture (FRAK-chur) the manner in which a mineral breaks if there is no cleavage

front (FRUNT) the boundary between two air masses

PRONUNCIATION KEY

CAPITAL LETTERS show the stressed syllables.

a	as in mat	f	as in fit
ay	as in day, say	g	as in go
ch	as in chew	i	as in sit
e	as in bed	j	as in job, gem
ee	as in even, easy, need	k	as in cool, key

frost (FROST) condensed water vapor, forming on surfaces with temperatures below freezing

full moon (FUL MOON) the phase of the Moon in which the entire disk is lighted and visible; the full moon occurs when Earth is directly between the Sun and the Moon.

gabbro (GA-broh) an igneous rock usually formed underground

galaxies (GA-luk-seez) large groups of stars held in gravitational orbit with one another

Galilean moons (ga-luh-LEE-un MOONZ) the four satellites of Jupiter seen by Galileo with his telescope; the Galilean moons are Io, Europa, Ganymede, and Callisto.

gas (GAS) the state of matter in which particles move quickly and can move beyond the confines of a container

gemstones (JEM-stohnz) valuable minerals, such as rubies or diamonds

geologic timetable (jee-uh-LO-jik TYM-tay-bul) chart that summarizes Earth's geologic history created by using absolute and relative ages of fossils and rocks found throughout Earth's crust

geology (jee-O-luh-jee) the study of Earth's crust and its interior

geyser (GY-zur) heated groundwater that rises to the surface of Earth and forms an erupting fountain, often on a repeating cycle

gibbous moon (GI-bus MOON) the phase of the Moon between the quarter and full, during which the Moon is shaped like a slightly oblong oval

---

PRONUNCIATION KEY

CAPITAL LETTERS show the stressed syllables.

ng as in runni**ng**	u as in b**u**t, s**o**me
o as in c**o**t, f**a**ther	uh as in **a**bout, tak**e**n, lem**o**n, penc**i**l
oh as in g**o**, n**o**te	ur as in t**er**m
sh as in **sh**y	y as in l**i**ne, fl**y**
th as in **th**in	zh as in vi**s**ion, mea**s**ure
oo as in t**oo**	

glacier (GLAY-shur) a large moving body of ice

global warming (GLOH-bul WOHR-ming) a period of average temperature increases, usually between ice ages

gneiss (NYS) a rock formed when granite is exposed to heat and pressure

gorges (GORJ-ez) steep-sided river valleys

granite (GRA-nut) a common igneous rock, used widely in building

gravity (GRA-vuh-tee) the force that attracts objects with mass to one another

Great Red Spot (GRAYT RED SPOT) on the surface of Jupiter, a large oval storm system that was first seen by Galileo

greenhouse effect (GREEN-hows i-FEKT) the trapping of heat near the surface of Earth by certain gases

groundwater (GROWND-wo-tur) all water that is found underground

gulfs (GULFS) inlets from oceans; gulfs are salt water.

gullies (GU-leez) small valleys cut by fast-moving water, often high in the mountains

guyots (GEE-ohz) seamounts that are flat on top, like mesas

gyres (JYRZ) circular ocean currents

half-life (HAF-lyf) the time it takes for one half of the radioactive element in a sample to decay

high-pressure areas (HY-PRE-shur AR-ee-uhz) regions of high air pressure, usually entire air masses

---

PRONUNCIATION KEY

CAPITAL LETTERS show the stressed syllables.

a	as in mat	f	as in fit
ay	as in day, say	g	as in go
ch	as in chew	i	as in sit
e	as in bed	j	as in job, gem
ee	as in even, easy, need	k	as in cool, key

hot spots (HOT SPOTS) areas of intense heat in the center of a plate that can burn through the lithosphere, creating volcanoes and island chains

hot springs (HOT SPRINGZ) heated groundwater that rises to the surface and forms hot pools

humidity (hyoo-MI-duh-tee) the amount of moisture in the atmosphere

hurricane (HUR-uh-kayn) the most severe type of tropical storm, with winds of at least 119 km/hr

hydrocarbons (HY-droh-kar-bunz) combinations of hydrogen and carbon; hydrocarbons are the byproducts of decaying material.

hydrologic cycle (hy-druh-LO-jik SY-kul) the process of evaporation of surface waters and the eventual return of surface waters to the ocean

hydrosphere (HY-droh-sfir) all the water in the atmosphere, on the surface, in groundwater, and bound in glaciers

ice age (YS AYJ) a period of extreme global cooling, in which ice sheets cover much of the temperate zones

ice cave (YS KAYV) a cave formed by glacial meltwater that pours from the opening

icebergs (YS-burgz) chunks of a glacier that have split off into the sea

igneous (IG-nee-us) rock formed from magma, or molten rock

index fossils (IN-deks FO-sulz) fossils of animals or plants that lived a short time throughout a wide area of the world; if an index fossil is found, geologists know the relative age of the rock layer.

PRONUNCIATION KEY

CAPITAL LETTERS show the stressed syllables.

ng as in running	u as in but, some
o as in cot, father	uh as in about, taken, lemon, pencil
oh as in go, note	ur as in term
sh as in shy	y as in line, fly
th as in thin	zh as in vision, measure
oo as in too	

inner core (I-nur KOHR) the innermost layer of Earth; the inner core is composed of solid iron and nickel.

inorganic (i-nor-GA-nik) being of matter other than plant or animal

intrusive rocks (in-TROO-siv ROKS) magma that cools while underground

ionosphere (y-O-nuh-sfir) a region in the upper stratosphere and lower mesosphere where radio transmissions can be affected by the solar radiation

irregular galaxies (i-RE-gyuh-lur GA-luk-seez) galaxies with no defined shape

irrigating (ir-uh-GAY-ting) using groundwater to water crops

isobars (Y-suh-barz) on a weather map, closed curves that define an area of equal air pressure

isolines (Y-soh-lynz) lines on a topographic map that connect points of equal elevation

jet streams (JET STREEMZ) strong rivers of wind that flow through the upper troposphere

Jovian (JOH-vee-un) related to Jupiter; in astronomy, a planet with a gas surface. The Jovian planets are Jupiter, Saturn, Uranus, and Neptune.

kettle lakes (KE-tul LAYKS) lakes formed within the drift of a retreating glacier

laccolith (LA-kuh-lith) a dome-shaped formation of hardened magma

---

PRONUNCIATION KEY

CAPITAL LETTERS show the stressed syllables.

a	as in mat	f	as in fit
ay	as in day, say	g	as in go
ch	as in chew	i	as in sit
e	as in bed	j	as in job, gem
ee	as in even, easy, need	k	as in cool, key

latitude (LA-tuh-tood) the distance in degrees north and south from Earth's equator

lava (LA-vuh) magma that has reached the surface of Earth, usually through volcanic activity

levees (LE-veez) built-up banks that contain river water even when the level rises above the level of the flood plain

lightning (LYT-ning) a static electricity discharge within clouds during a thunderstorm

light-year (LYT-yir) the distance light travels in one year

limestone (LYM-stohn) a sedimentary rock formed from the shells of living organisms

liquid (LI-kwud) the state of matter in which particles are not arranged in any particular way, and the material takes on the shape of its container

lithosphere (LI-thuh-sfir) the crust and upper mantle of Earth, where all solid rock exists

Local Group (LOH-kul GROOP) a cluster of galaxies held together by gravitational attraction; our galaxy, the Milky Way, is one of the Local Group.

longitude (LON-juh-tood) the distance in degrees of any point east or west from the prime meridian

low-pressure areas (LOH-PRE-shur AR-ee-uhz) regions where the air pressure is low, usually along fronts where two air masses come together

luster (LUS-tur) the way light reflects from a mineral

PRONUNCIATION KEY

CAPITAL LETTERS show the stressed syllables.

ng	as in running	u	as in but, some
o	as in cot, father	uh	as in about, taken, lemon, pencil
oh	as in go, note	ur	as in term
sh	as in shy	y	as in line, fly
th	as in thin	zh	as in vision, measure
oo	as in too		

L wave (EL WAYV) wave created when P waves and S waves reach the surface; L waves move the ground up, down, and sideways.

mafic magma (MA-fik MAG-muh) dark, thin magma, low in silicate content

magma (MAG-muh) molten rock

magma chamber (MAG-muh CHAYM-bur) a pocket of hot magma that collects below the surface of the volcanic mountain

magnetic declination (mag-NE-tik de-kluh-NAY-shun) the difference between true north and the magnetic north pole

magnetosphere (mag-NEE-tuh-sfir) Earth's magnetic force field

mantle (MAN-tul) the second layer of Earth from the surface; the upper mantle is plastic and moves in convection cells.

map projections (MAP pruh-JEK-shunz) maps that show the globe or an area on it as it would appear projected onto a flat surface

map scale (MAP SKAYL) a method for showing how the measurement of the map relates to the measurement of real Earth

marble (MAR-bul) a rock that limestone becomes when it is exposed to contact with hot magma

maria (MAR-ee-uh) the "seas" on the Moon, made of darker lava

maritime air mass (MAR-uh-tym AR MAS) an air mass that forms over water

maxima (MAK-suh-muh) the time during the 11-year sunspot cycle when there are the largest number of sunspots

---

PRONUNCIATION KEY

CAPITAL LETTERS show the stressed syllables.

a	as in mat	f	as in fit
ay	as in day, say	g	as in go
ch	as in chew	i	as in sit
e	as in bed	j	as in job, gem
ee	as in even, easy, need	k	as in cool, key

meanders (mee-AN-durz) the paths a mature river takes, moving in a side-to-side fashion

mechanical weathering (mi-KA-ni-kul WETH-ring) the breaking apart of rocks due to rain, wind, and so forth

meltwater (MELT-wo-tur) water that melts from snow and glaciers

Mercator projection (mur-KAY-tur pruh-JEK-shun) a flat map in which meridians become parallel lines

meridians (muh-RI-dee-unz) lines of longitude

mesopause (ME-zuh-poz) the boundary between the mesosphere and the thermosphere

mesosphere (ME-zuh-sfir) the region of the atmosphere above the stratosphere and below the thermosphere

metals (ME-tulz) a group of elements known for their ability to reflect light in a particular way; gold, silver, and iron are metals.

metamorphic (me-tuh-MOR-fik) rock that is changed in form because of heat or pressure

meteor (MEE-tee-ur) a meteoroid that has fallen into the atmosphere of Earth

meteorite (MEE-tee-uh-ryt) a meteor that has crashed onto Earth's surface

meteoroids (MEE-tee-uh-royds) bodies of rock or metal that are debris left over from the formation of the solar system; some are tiny, and some are several kilometers in diameter.

PRONUNCIATION KEY

CAPITAL LETTERS show the stressed syllables.

ng as in runni**ng**	u as in b**u**t, s**o**me
o as in c**o**t, f**a**ther	uh as in **a**bout, tak**e**n, lem**o**n, penc**i**l
oh as in g**o**, n**o**te	ur as in t**er**m
sh as in **sh**y	y as in l**i**ne, fl**y**
th as in **th**in	zh as in vi**s**ion, mea**s**ure
oo as in t**oo**	

meteorology (mee-tee-uh-RO-luh-jee) the study of the atmosphere and weather

millibars (MI-luh-barz) metric units for measuring air pressure

mineral cast (MIN-rul KAST) a fossil in which the organic material decays slowly, leaving a mold; if future minerals fill in the mold, the result is a mineral cast.

mineral mold (MIN-rul MOHLD) hole left in rock in the original shape of a plant or an animal after the original remains decay completely

mineral ore (MIN-rul OR) any rock that contains a metal

mineral remains (MIN-rul ri-MAYNS) a fossil in which minerals seep in and eventually replace the decaying organic matter; a piece of petrified wood is an example.

minima (MI-nuh-muh) the time during the 11-year sunspot cycle when there are the fewest sunspots

minutes (MI-nuts) a division of degrees, used for greater accuracy in noting latitude and longitude

mixed layer (MIKST LAY-ur) the layer of the oceans where light penetrates and most ocean organisms live

molecules (MO-li-kyoolz) combinations of two or more atoms

monsoon winds (mon-SOON WINDZ) seasonal winds that change direction, changing the weather as they go

moraines (muh-RAYNZ) pieces of rock that have fallen from a valley wall and been carried by a glacier

---

PRONUNCIATION KEY

CAPITAL LETTERS show the stressed syllables.

a	as in mat	f	as in fit
ay	as in day, say	g	as in go
ch	as in chew	i	as in sit
e	as in bed	j	as in job, gem
ee	as in even, easy, need	k	as in cool, key

mountain glaciers (MOWN-tun GLAY-shurz) glaciers that lie in a mountain valley and can be hundreds of meters thick; they are only found at the highest elevations.

neap tides (NEEP TYDZ) the lowest tides, when the Sun's and the Moon's gravity is at opposition

new moon (NOO MOON) the phase of the Moon during which the Moon is not visible to an observer on Earth; the new moon occurs when the Moon is between Earth and the Sun.

nimbostratus (nim-boh-STRA-tus) describes thick, heavy clouds close to Earth's surface that bring steady rain

Northern Hemisphere (NOR-thurn HE-muh-sfir) the northern half of Earth

nuclear fusion (NOO-klee-ur FYOO-zhun) the process of fusing hydrogen into helium

obsidian (ub-SI-dee-un) an igneous rock that cooled very quickly, so there was no time for crystals to grow; obsidian was often used as arrowheads, and it is known as "volcanic glass."

occluded front (uh-KLOOD-ed FRUNT) a front in which a warm air mass is wedged between two cold air masses

ocean current (OH-shun KUR-unt) a wide area of ocean water that flows continuously

ocean ridges (OH-shun RIJ-ez) undersea mountain ranges

PRONUNCIATION KEY

CAPITAL LETTERS show the stressed syllables.

ng as in running	u as in but, some
o as in cot, father	uh as in about, taken, lemon, pencil
oh as in go, note	ur as in term
sh as in shy	y as in line, fly
th as in thin	zh as in vision, measure
oo as in too	

ocean trenches (OH-shun TRENCH-ez) the deepest parts of the ocean basin

oceanic crust (oh-shee-A-nik KRUST) the crust below Earth's oceans, which is thinner than the continental crust

oceanography (oh-shuh-NO-gruh-fee) the study of Earth's oceans

oceans (OH-shunz) the large bodies of salt water that surround the continents

Oort cloud (OHRT KLOWD) a collection of celestial debris in the outer solar system, beyond the orbit of Pluto; it is from here some comets are dislodged and fall toward the Sun.

orbit (OR-but) the path an object takes around another

orbital period (OR-buh-tul PIR-ee-ud) the length of time it takes a comet to make a complete journey around the Sun and return; orbital periods can be many years long.

organic (or-GA-nik) related to living organisms; for example, organic sedimentary rock is formed from the shells of living things.

outer core (OW-tur KOHR) the third layer of Earth from the surface; the outer core is made of molten iron and gives rise to Earth's magnetic field

outwash (OWT-wosh) deposits of rocky material left by glacial meltwater

oxbow lakes (OKS-boh LAYKS) small lakes formed by the connection of two sides of a meander

ozone layer (OH-zohn LAY-ur) a region in the upper troposphere and

---

PRONUNCIATION KEY

CAPITAL LETTERS show the stressed syllables.

a	as in mat	f	as in fit
ay	as in day, say	g	as in go
ch	as in chew	i	as in sit
e	as in bed	j	as in job, gem
ee	as in even, easy, need	k	as in cool, key

lower stratosphere in which ozone collects as a result of solar radiation; the ozone layer scatters ultraviolet radiation and keeps Earth safe for life.

Pangaea (pan-JEE-uh) the large landmass in Earth's remote past that contained all the modern continents

parallels (PAR-uh-lelz) lines of latitude

penumbra (puh-NUM-bruh) a partial shadow during an eclipse

perigee (PER-uh-jee) the position where the Moon is closest to Earth

perihelion (per-uh-HEEL-yun) the position of Earth when it is closest to the Sun

periods (PIR-ee-udz) divisions of geologic time that are longer than an epoch and included in an era

permeable (PUR-mee-uh-bul) type of soil through which water can flow

petroleum (puh-TROH-lee-um) an oily liquid obtained from the ground that is a source of gasoline, fuel oils, and other products

phases (FAY-zez) daily changes in the Moon's or an inferior planet's appearance

photosphere (FOH-tuh-sfir) the outer layer of the Sun, which is the only visible part to an observer on Earth most of the time

planetary winds (PLA-nuh-ter-ee WINDZ) winds that circulate heat and moisture throughout the entire troposphere

plate tectonics (PLAYT tek-TO-niks) the theory that Earth has several large plates that move around the planet because of motion from the upper mantle

PRONUNCIATION KEY

CAPITAL LETTERS show the stressed syllables.

ng	as in running	u	as in but, some
o	as in cot, father	uh	as in about, taken, lemon, pencil
oh	as in go, note	ur	as in term
sh	as in shy	y	as in line, fly
th	as in thin	zh	as in vision, measure
oo	as in too		

polar air mass (POH-lur AR MAS) air mass formed in regions between 60° north and the North Pole, or 60° south and the South Pole

Polaris (puh-LAR-us) the star toward which the northern end of Earth's axis nearly points; also called the North Star

polarity (poh-LAR-uh-tee) the north or south orientation of Earth's magnetic field; currently, the field is oriented toward the north.

polyconic projection (po-lee-KO-nik pruh-JEK-shun) a flat map that has greater accuracy at the poles than the Mercator projection

porous rock (POHR-us ROK) rock that has gaps between its particles

precipitation (pri-si-puh-TAY-shun) moisture that falls from the sky in the form of rain, sleet, hail, or snow

pressure gradient (PRE-shur GRAY-dee-unt) the rate at which air pressure changes

prevailing winds (pri-VAY-ling WINDZ) ground-level winds that occur in a wind belt across the globe

prime meridian (PRYM muh-RI-dee-un) the line of longitude that runs from the North Pole to the South Pole through Greenwich, England

pulsar (PUL-sar) a collapsed star that sends out energy in pulses as it rotates; it is also called a neutron star.

pumice (PUH-mus) an igneous rock formed with so much gas that the rock is light enough to float in water

P wave (PEE WAYV) the primary wave in an earthquake; it can move through any material.

PRONUNCIATION KEY

CAPITAL LETTERS show the stressed syllables.

a	as in mat	f	as in fit
ay	as in day, say	g	as in go
ch	as in chew	i	as in sit
e	as in bed	j	as in job, gem
ee	as in even, easy, need	k	as in cool, key

quarter moon (KWOR-tur MOON) the phase of the Moon during which the Moon appears to be a half-moon shape

quartzite (KWORT-syt) a metamorphic rock made from sandstone

quasars (KWAY-zarz) starlike objects that give off strong radio signals

radiative zone (RAY-dee-ay-tiv ZOHN) region near the core of the Sun where high-energy particles pass

radio telescopes (RAY-dee-oh TE-luh-skohps) telescopes that gather energy in the form of radio waves

radioactive decay (ray-dee-oh-AK-tiv di-KAY) the breaking down of elements into other stable elements over time; radioactive decay gives off heat, which is one reason the interior of the planet is hotter than the surface.

radiometric dating (ray-dee-oh-ME-trik DAY-ting) determining the age of a fossil based on the rate of decay of radioactive elements contained within it

rapids (RA-pudz) part of a river formed over steep ground and large rocks where water flows quickly enough to bubble and churn

red giant (RED JY-unt) a star near the end of its life whose core has collapsed, sending its temperature zooming

redshift (RED-SHIFT) a shift in light or energy that demonstrates that an object is moving away from the observer

reflecting telescope (ri-FLEK-ting TE-luh-skohp) a telescope that uses mirrors to gather light

---

PRONUNCIATION KEY

CAPITAL LETTERS show the stressed syllables.

ng	as in running	u	as in but, some
o	as in cot, father	uh	as in about, taken, lemon, pencil
oh	as in go, note	ur	as in term
sh	as in shy	y	as in line, fly
th	as in thin	zh	as in vision, measure
oo	as in too		

refracting telescope (ri-FRAK-ting TE-luh-skohp) a telescope that uses lenses to gather light

regional metamorphism (REEJ-nul me-tuh-MOR-fi-zum) changes that occur in rock because of heat and pressure over a large area

relative age (RE-luh-tiv AYJ) the age of a fossil compared with the other fossils in the strata

relative humidity (RE-luh-tiv hyoo-MI-duh-tee) the amount of moisture in the atmosphere, relative to the amount the atmosphere can hold

renewable resources (ri-NOO-uh-bul REE-sor-sez) energy sources that can be replaced, such as wood, or do not need replacing, such as solar and wind

retreat (ri-TREET) the recession of a glacier during the warm season

revolves (ri-VOLVZ) moves in a curved path round a center; orbits

rhyolite (RY-uh-lyt) a glassy, fine-grained igneous rock

Richter scale (RIK-tur SKAYL) the scale used to measure earthquakes; the Richter scale is logarithmic, which means that an earthquake that measures 7 on the scale is ten times stronger than an earthquake that measures 6 on the scale.

rift (RIFT) any region, on dry continents or underwater, where the plates seem to be pulling away from each other

rift zones (RIFT ZOHNZ) regions where plates move slowly away from each other

---

PRONUNCIATION KEY

CAPITAL LETTERS show the stressed syllables.

a	as in mat	f	as in fit
ay	as in day, say	g	as in go
ch	as in chew	i	as in sit
e	as in bed	j	as in job, gem
ee	as in even, easy, need	k	as in cool, key

rings (RINGZ) collections of chunky rocks and ice that orbit a planet and appear to be a solid ring of material; all four Jovian planets have ring systems.

rivers (RI-vurz) moving bodies of surface water that have their origins in the mountains and flow to the sea

river system (RI-vur SIS-tum) system made up of a river and its tributaries

rock cycle (ROK SY-kul) the process through which rocks change from igneous to other forms and are melted back into magma

rotates (ROH-tayts) spins on an axis

runoff (RUN-of) rainwater that rolls off the land without soaking in and is carried back to the ocean in streams and rivers

salinity (suh-LI-nuh-tee) the measure of the dissolved solids in water

saltwater intrusion (SOLT-wo-tur in-TROO-zhun) contamination of groundwater by ocean water

sandstone (SAND-stohn) a sedimentary rock formed from grains of sand cemented together

satellite (SA-tul-yt) an object that orbits a planet; a satellite can be natural, such as a moon, or artificial, such as a space station.

saturated (sa-chuh-RAY-tud) condition in which the atmosphere can hold no more water vapor

scattered (SKA-turd) describing energy spread randomly by collisions with particles in the atmosphere

---

PRONUNCIATION KEY

CAPITAL LETTERS show the stressed syllables.

ng	as in running	u	as in but, some
o	as in cot, father	uh	as in about, taken, lemon, pencil
oh	as in go, note	ur	as in term
sh	as in shy	y	as in line, fly
th	as in thin	zh	as in vision, measure
oo	as in too		

sea ice (SEE YS) a layer of ice that forms over ocean waters in extremely cold climates, normally around the poles

sea level (SEE LE-vul) the level of the surface of the sea especially at the point midway between the highest seas and the lowest seas; the lowest part of the atmosphere

seamounts (SEE-mownts) volcanic mountains located on the seafloor

seas (SEEZ) inlets from oceans; seas are salt water.

seafloor spreading (SEE-flor SPRE-ding) the movement of the plates away from one another on the seafloor, which leaves a characteristic pattern of magnetic polarity

sedimentary (se-duh-MEN-tuh-ree) rock formed from sediments such as sand or mud

seismic waves (SYZ-mik WAYVZ) any energy waves caused by an earthquake

seismograph (SYZ-muh-graf) an instrument used to detect and measure earthquake waves

shale (SHAYL) a sedimentary rock formed from clay and silt that has been tightly compacted

shield cone (SHEELD KOHN) formation with gently sloping sides formed when mafic magma rises through the lithosphere

silica (SI-li-kuh) a combination of the elements silicon and oxygen that is found in magma

---

PRONUNCIATION KEY

CAPITAL LETTERS show the stressed syllables.

a	as in mat		f	as in fit
ay	as in day, say		g	as in go
ch	as in chew		i	as in sit
e	as in bed		j	as in job, gem
ee	as in even, easy, need		k	as in cool, key

silicates (SI-luh-kayts) the mineral group that comprises most of the rocks on Earth

sill (SIL) a rock formation in which magma cuts horizontally across existing rocks

slate (SLAYT) a rock that shale becomes when exposed to heat and pressure

snout (SNOWT) the front edge of a glacier

snow line (SNOH LYN) the lowest elevation where mountain glaciers can begin to form

soil (SOYL) a mixture of weathered rock and organic material that contains minerals and nutrients that support plant life

solar energy (SOH-lur E-nur-jee) the energy from the Sun, including all forms of electromagnetic radiation

solar flares (SOH-lur FLARZ) explosions from sunspots that send waves of energy into space

solar prominences (SOH-lur PRO-muh-nunts-ez) huge loops, or arches of cooler gas, that rise through the corona of the Sun

solar wind (SOH-lur WIND) a stream of particles, mostly protons, that are constantly ejected from the Sun

solid (SO-lud) the state of matter in which particles are densely packed, and the material assumes its own shape independent of a container

solstice (SOL-stus) the point in the apparent path of the Sun where the Sun is farthest north or south of the equator

PRONUNCIATION KEY

CAPITAL LETTERS show the stressed syllables.

ng as in running	u as in but, some
o as in cot, father	uh as in about, taken, lemon, pencil
oh as in go, note	ur as in term
sh as in shy	y as in line, fly
th as in thin	zh as in vision, measure
oo as in too	

Southern Hemisphere (SUH-thurn HE-muh-sfir) the southern half of Earth

specific gravity (spi-SI-fik GRA-vuh-tee) the density of a mineral compared to water

specific heat (spi-SI-fik HEET) the amount of energy needed to raise the temperature of a material

specific humidity (spi-SI-fik hyoo-MI-duh-tee) the exact amount of moisture in the atmosphere

speed of light (SPEED UV LYT) 300,000 km per second

spiral galaxies (SPY-rul GA-luk-seez) galaxies with a pinwheel shape and usually two or more arms

spring tides (SPRING TYDZ) the highest tides, when the Sun's gravity and the Moon's gravity are combined

springs (SPRINGZ) places where groundwater spills out at the surface of Earth

squall line (SKWOL LYN) a series of thunderstorms organized in a line ahead of an approaching cold front

stalactites (stuh-LAK-tyts) calcite formations in caves; stalactites hang from the ceiling.

stalagmites (stuh-LAG-myts) calcite formations in caves; stalagmites grow from the floor.

stars (STARZ) giant balls of burning hydrogen gas, whose heat and light is caused by nuclear fusion

---

PRONUNCIATION KEY

CAPITAL LETTERS show the stressed syllables.

a	as in mat	f	as in fit
ay	as in day, say	g	as in go
ch	as in chew	i	as in sit
e	as in bed	j	as in job, gem
ee	as in even, easy, need	k	as in cool, key

stationary front (STAY-shuh-ner-ee FRUNT) a front in which the two air masses do not move for a long time

stratopause (STRA-toh-poz) the boundary between the stratosphere and the mesosphere

stratosphere (STRA-tuh-sfir) the region of the atmosphere above the troposphere and below the mesosphere

stratus (STRA-tus) describes low, gray sheets of clouds that completely cover the sky

streak (STREEK) the color of a mineral's powder when rubbed on a white tile; used to help identify minerals

streams (STREEMZ) moving bodies of surface water

subduction zones (sub-DUK-shun ZOHNZ) regions where one plate is being pulled down under another

sublimation (suh-bluh-MAY-shun) the passing of a solid into a gas without moving first through the liquid state of matter

submarine canyons (SUB-muh-reen KAN-yuns) wide underwater gullies

subsidence (SUB-suh-duns) the sinking of land as groundwater is mined

sunspots (SUN-spots) magnetic storms on the surface of the Sun; from Earth, they look like dark spots.

supernova (soo-pur-NOH-vuh) an explosion triggered by the collapse of a very massive star

superposition (soo-pur-puh-ZI-shun) the law that states that in undisturbed rock layers, the oldest rock is always on the bottom

---

PRONUNCIATION KEY

CAPITAL LETTERS show the stressed syllables.

ng as in runni**ng**	u as in b**u**t, s**o**me
o as in c**o**t, f**a**ther	uh as in **a**bout, tak**e**n, lem**o**n, penc**i**l
oh as in g**o**, n**o**te	ur as in t**er**m
sh as in **sh**y	y as in l**i**ne, fl**y**
th as in **th**in	zh as in vi**s**ion, mea**s**ure
oo as in t**oo**	

surface current (SUR-fus KUR-unt) ocean current that flows horizontally across the ocean's surface

S wave (ES WAYV) the second wave in an earthquake; it can only move through solid ground.

telescope (TE-luh-skohp) a device for gathering starlight and other energy forms from celestial objects

temperate (TEM-puh-rut) relating to events between 30° north and 60° north, or 30° south and 60° south; characterized by cold or cool winters and warm summers

temperature (TEM-puh-chur) the measure of the heat of air particles

temperature inversion (TEM-puh-chur in-VUR-zhun) colder temperatures at ground level than in the sky; precipitation during a temperature inversion is likely to be freezing rain or sleet.

terminal moraine (TUR-muh-nul muh-RAYN) the end moraine that is left behind by the farthest advance of a glacier

terrestrial (tuh-RES-tree-ul) related to Earth; in astronomy, a planet with a rocky surface. The terrestrial planets are Mercury, Venus, Earth, Mars, and Pluto.

thermocline (THUR-muh-klyn) the region in the ocean below the mixed layer, where the temperature drops rapidly

thermometer (thur-MO-muh-tur) an instrument for measuring temperature

---

PRONUNCIATION KEY

CAPITAL LETTERS show the stressed syllables.

a	as in m**at**	f	as in **f**it
ay	as in d**ay**, s**ay**	g	as in **g**o
ch	as in **ch**ew	i	as in s**i**t
e	as in b**e**d	j	as in **j**ob, **g**em
ee	as in **e**ven, **ea**sy, n**ee**d	k	as in **c**ool, **k**ey

thermosphere (THUR-muh-sfir) the region of the atmosphere above the mesosphere and below outer space

thunder (THUN-dur) the sound of air expanding as lightning burns a path through it

thunderstorms (THUN-dur-stormz) common storms formed in cumulonimbus clouds and characterized by electrical activity

tides (TYDZ) the rising and falling of surface water in response to the gravitational pull of the Moon and the Sun

till (TIL) deposits of the rocky materials carried directly by a glacier

topographic (to-puh-GRA-fik) type of map that shows the vertical distances of a landscape, such as hills and valleys

tornado (tor-NAY-doh) a spinning updraft of wind, usually associated with thunderstorms; tornados are extremely powerful wind events and can destroy buildings.

totality (toh-TA-luh-tee) the phase of an eclipse when light is completely blocked

trace fossils (TRAYS FO-sulz) impressions left by plants or animals, for instance, leaf imprints left in mud

trade winds (TRAYD WINDZ) the prevailing winds between the equator and the 30° latitudes

transform fault (TRANS-form FOLT) a fault where two plates slide past each other

transpiration (trans-puh-RAY-shun) the water vapor given off by plants

---

PRONUNCIATION KEY

CAPITAL LETTERS show the stressed syllables.

ng	as in running	u	as in but, some
o	as in cot, father	uh	as in about, taken, lemon, pencil
oh	as in go, note	ur	as in term
sh	as in shy	y	as in line, fly
th	as in thin	zh	as in vision, measure
oo	as in too		

tributaries (TRI-byuh-ter-eez) streams or small rivers that join with large rivers

trilobites (TRY-luh-byts) hard-shelled crablike organisms that lived in the oceans during most of the Paleozoic Era

tropical air mass (TRO-pi-kul AR MAS) air mass formed in regions between 30° north and 30° south and covering the equatorial region

tropical depression (TRO-pi-kul di-PRE-shun) a low-pressure center in which warm air rises and condenses to form cumulonimbus clouds

tropical storm (TRO-pi-kul STORM) a tropical depression that drops precipitation

tropopause (TROH-puh-poz) the boundary between the troposphere and the stratosphere

troposphere (TROH-puh-sfir) the lowest layer of the atmosphere, where weather occurs

trough (TROF) the bottom of a wave

true north (TROO NORTH) the geographic north pole

tsunami (soo-NO-mee) a seismic wave, triggered by an underwater earthquake, that can reach heights of many meters once it reaches the shore

turbidity currents (tur-BI-duh-tee KUR-unts) undersea landslides, often caused by an earthquake

umbra (UM-bruh) the completely dark portion of the shadow during an eclipse

---

PRONUNCIATION KEY

CAPITAL LETTERS show the stressed syllables.

a	as in m**a**t	f	as in **f**it
ay	as in d**ay**, s**ay**	g	as in **g**o
ch	as in **ch**ew	i	as in s**i**t
e	as in b**e**d	j	as in **j**ob, **g**em
ee	as in **e**ven, **ea**sy, n**ee**d	k	as in **c**ool, **k**ey

uniform gases (YOO-nuh-form GAS-ez) gases such as nitrogen that do not vary significantly in the atmosphere

upwelling (up-WE-ling) a current that flows from the ocean bottom to the surface, bringing with it nutrients from the seafloor

uranium dating (yoo-RAY-nee-um DAY-ting) a radiometric dating technique using uranium-238 that can find the age of Earth's oldest rocks

vacuum (VA-kyoom) a space with no particles of matter within it; outer space is a near vacuum.

variable gases (VER-ee-uh-bul GAS-ez) gases such as carbon dioxide that change significantly in the atmosphere

vent (VENT) in a volcano, the opening at the top of the cone through which magma is released

vertical currents (VUR-ti-kul KUR-unts) ocean currents that flow vertically through the ocean's layers

volcanic mountains (vol-KA-nik MOWN-tunz) cone-shaped mountains built up from layers of lava, often found along subduction zones

volcanic outgassing (vol-KA-nik OWT-gas-sing) the means by which the early atmosphere was created; volcanoes issued nitrogen, carbon dioxide, and water vapor.

volcanoes (vol-KAY-nohz) openings in the ground through which magma flows

waning moon (WAY-ning MOON) moon that is steadily growing smaller in appearance

---

PRONUNCIATION KEY

CAPITAL LETTERS show the stressed syllables.

ng	as in runni**ng**	u	as in b**u**t, s**o**me
o	as in c**o**t, f**a**ther	uh	as in **a**bout, tak**e**n, lem**o**n, penc**i**l
oh	as in g**o**, n**o**te	ur	as in t**er**m
sh	as in **sh**y	y	as in l**i**ne, fl**y**
th	as in **th**in	zh	as in vi**s**ion, mea**s**ure
oo	as in t**oo**		

warm front (WOHRM FRUNT) a front in which the warm air mass moves more quickly than the cold air mass

warm water vents (WOHRM WO-tur VENTS) vents of warm water from the mantle, near the mid-ocean ridges; the warm water vents provide a habitat for certain organisms.

water cycle (WO-tur SY-kul) another term for the hydrologic cycle; the means by which Earth's water is continually recycled

water table (WO-tur TAY-bul) the top level of the groundwater

waterfall (WO-tur-fol) a fall of water, usually from a great height

watershed (WO-tur-shed) a drainage basin

wave (WAYV) the means by which energy travels; waves have crests and troughs, and a definite wavelength.

wave height (WAYV HYT) the measurement of a wave from crest to trough

wavelength (WAYV-length) the length of a wave from crest to crest

waxing moon (WAK-sing MOON) moon that is steadily growing larger in appearance

weather (WE-thur) the day-to-day change that takes place in the troposphere

weathering (WE-thuh-ring) the breaking apart of materials at or near Earth's surface due to rain, wind, freezing, and thawing

westerlies (WES-tur-leez) the prevailing winds in the temperate latitudes

---

PRONUNCIATION KEY

CAPITAL LETTERS show the stressed syllables.

a	as in m**a**t	f	as in **f**it
ay	as in d**ay**, s**ay**	g	as in **g**o
ch	as in **ch**ew	i	as in s**i**t
e	as in b**e**d	j	as in **j**ob, **g**em
ee	as in **e**ven, **ea**sy, n**ee**d	k	as in **c**ool, **k**ey

white dwarf (WYT DWORF) a star at the end of its life whose core has collapsed; it gives off a little heat and light, until it cools down.

wind chill factor (WIND CHIL FAK-tur) the temperature the air actually feels like due to wind

wind shear (WIND SHIR) wind event in which the wind blows across the top of a cloud in one direction and across the bottom in another direction

zone of aeration (ZOHN UV ar-AY-shun) the region above the water table, where air is between soil particles

zone of saturation (ZOHN UV sa-chuh-RAY-shun) the region below the water table, where the soil is wet

---

PRONUNCIATION KEY

CAPITAL LETTERS show the stressed syllables.

ng	as in running	u	as in but, some
o	as in cot, father	uh	as in about, taken, lemon, pencil
oh	as in go, note	ur	as in term
sh	as in shy	y	as in line, fly
th	as in thin	zh	as in vision, measure
oo	as in too		

INDEX

aa, 139
absolute age, 149
absolute magnitude, 15
abyssal hills, 176
abyssal plains, 176
acid rain, 132, 205
advance, 192
African Plate, 145
aftershocks, 143
air
    circulating in convection cell, 80
    contraction of, 64
    expansion of, 63
    heating of, 63–64, 80
    particles, 63, 65–66
    weight of, 102–103
air masses, 85–87
    boundary between two, 87. *See also*
      fronts
    continental, 85
    maritime, 85
    polar, 85, 86
    tropical, 85, 86
    types of, 86
air pressure, 67–68
    and altitude, 68
    expression of, 67
    temperature and, 65–68
alluvial fans, 188
Alps, 193, 194
Altair, 45
altitude
    air pressure and, 68
    effect on climate of, 94
    temperature changes with, 57–58
altostratus clouds, 74, 87–88
Andes Mountains, 137, 146
Andromeda Galaxy, 12
Antarctica, 173, 179
Antarctic Circle, 42
anthracite, 127
aphelion, 40

apogee, 32
***Apollo 9* mission,** 31
Appalachian Mountains, 145
apparent magnitude, 15
applications
    change in matter and ability to float,
      154–155
    creating model of volcanic activity,
      155–156
    glacial flow, 209–211
    gravitational force and planetary orbit,
      48–49
    heating Earth's surface, 100–101
    mystery boulders, 211
    relating distance and apparent motion,
      50–51
    sediments, 156–157
    water wear, 208–209
    weight of air, 102–103
aquifers, 198–199, 200
Aquila, 45
Arctic Circle, 42
Arctic Ocean, 171, 173, 179
artesian formations, 199–200
artesian wells, 200
ash, 139
asterisms, 44
asteroids, 17, 28–29
asthenosphere, 135
    hot spots in, 140
astronomers, 4
    beliefs of ancient, 39
    use of radio telescopes by, 8
astronomical unit (AU), 40
astronomy, 4
Atlantic Ocean, 171, 173, 185
    size of, 172
atmosphere
    complexity of weather in, 89
    evaporation and condensation in, 70
    of gas, 63–64
    greenhouse gases in, 62

heating of, by ground, 61, 62
increase of carbon dioxide in, 96
of Mars, 22
mesosphere, 59
of Neptune, 26
origins of, 55–56
protection from, 57
stratosphere, 58–59
of Sun, 18
thermosphere, 59
of Titan, 26
today, 56
troposphere, 58
of Venus, 22
warmth of, 60–62
water in, 69
winds in, 77–84
atolls, 177
atoms, 163
aurora, 19
Aurora Australis, 19
Aurora Borealis, 19
axis
of Earth, 40, 41
of Mercury, 21

bacteria
entry into water supplies of, 205
first appearance of, 56
Baltic Sea, 172–173
barometers, 67
basalt, 124, 139, 141, 183
batholiths, 124
bays, 171
beaches, 183
bed, 186
bed load, 186
bedrock, 167, 200
Betelgeuse, 16, 45
Big Bang theory, 9–10
Big Crunch, 10
Big Dipper, 44
binary stars, 15
bituminous, 127

black holes, 11, 14
blue supergiants, 45
bombs, 139
bonds, 164
breakers, 183

calcite, 167, 201
caldera, 139, 140
Callisto, 26
Canary Current, 179
canyons, 187
cap rock, 199–200
carbon, 130
carbon-14, 150
carbon dating, 150
carbon dioxide, 96
carbonic acid, 167
in rainwater, 201
Cascade Range, 140, 146
caverns, underground, 201
caves, underground, 201
Celsius scale, 66
Cepheid variables, 15
Ceres, 28–29
Charon, 23
chemical sedimentary rocks, 127
chemical weathering, 167, 201
Chesapeake Bay, 189, 205
chlorofluorocarbons (CFCs), 59
chromosphere, 18
during solar eclipse, 36
cinder cones, 140
circumpolar constellations, 44–45
cirque, 194
cirque horn, 194
cirrocumulous clouds, 74
cirrostratus clouds, 74, 87
cirrus clouds, 74, 88
heralding warm front, 87
clastic sedimentary rocks, 126
clay, 183, 197
cleavage, 121
climate
change, 96–97

deposition, 165, 189
dew, 70, 71
    formation of, 72
dew point, 71
dikes, 124
dinosaurs, extinction of, 151
divides, 185
doldrums, 83
dome mountains, 146
downdrafts, 91
drainage basin, 185
drift, 194
drizzle, 75
drumlins, 195

Earth
    continental crust, 108
    crust, 108
    distance from Sun of, 17
    energy budget of, 61
    fossil record of, 147–149
    geologic timetable of, 151–152, 215
    as a globe, 112–114
    heating surface of, 100–101
    importance of atmosphere to, 55
    importance of Sun to, 20
    inner core, 109
    inside, 108–109
    internal heat of, 109–110
    as a magnet, 110–111
    mantle, 109
    mapping, 114–115
    naturally occurring elements on, 108
    oceanic crust, 108
    orbit of, around Sun, 4, 39–40
    outer core, 109
    reason for layers of, 109
    similarities between Mars and, 23
    surface and interior of, 107–110
    three temperature zones of, 94
    tilted axis of, 40, 41
earthquakes, 4, 141–144
    aftershocks of, 143
    underwater, 144

earth science
    areas of, 4–5
    defined, 4
eclipses, 35–37
    lunar eclipse, 36–37
    solar eclipse, 35–36
    totality, during solar, 36
electromagnetic spectrum, 6
electromagnetic waves, 6
elements, 108
    creation of, 14
    of water, 163
elevation, 117
elliptical galaxies, 12
El Niño, 4, 180
    climate changes cause by, 94
energy
    delivered to Earth in form of light, 61
    from hurricanes, 93
    resources of fossil fuels, 131–132
    sources, alternative, 97, 132
energy budget, 61
epicenter, of earthquake, 142
epochs, 151
equator
    doldrums, at, 83
    length of days and nights at, 41
    slight bulge of Earth at, 107
    snow line at, 191
eras, 151
    in geologic timetable chart, 215
erosion, 129, 185
    defined, 166
    necessity of plant life to protect soil
      from, 167
    rainwater, as agent of, 187
    strongest agent of, 186
    weathering and, 166–168
erratic, 195
eskers, 195
estuaries, 189
Eurasian Plate, 145
Europa, 25
eutrophication, 205

evaporation, 70, 164
  freshwater supplied by, 169
expansion, 63
exquinoxes, 42–43
extraterrestrial beings, search for signals
  from, 8
extrusive rocks, 123
eye, of hurricane, 92

Fahrenheit scale, 66
fall equinox, 43
fault-block mountains, 146
faults, 136
  examples of, 137
felsic magma, 124, 139
fertilizers, 204
Finger Lakes, 195
firn, 191
floodplains, 189
floods, 4
focus, of earthquake, 142
fog, 70, 71
  formation of, 72
fold mountains, 145
fossil fuels, 130–131
  advantage of, 131–132
  burning of, 96
  limited supply of, 132
fossils, 147
  formation of, 147–148
  relative and absolute age of, 149
fracture, 121
freezing, 164
freezing rain, 75
freshwater, 169
  sea ice made of, 173
friction, heat created by, 110
fronts, 87
  cold, 88
  low-pressure centers developing along,
    88
  occluded, 88
  polar, 88–89
  stationary, 88

warm, 87
frost, 70
  formation of, 72
full moon, 34

gabbro, 125
galaxies, 10–12
  Andromeda Galaxy, 12
  elliptical, 12
  irregular, 12
  Local Group, 12
  Milky Way Galaxy, 10, 11, 12, 14
  spiral, 11–12
  types of, 11–12
Galilean moons, 25–26
Galileo, 7
  naming of maria by, 32
gamma rays, 6, 8
Ganymede, 26
gases
  atmosphere of, 63–64
  greenhouse, 62
  uniform, 56
  variable, 56, 62
gasoline, 96
gemstones, 120
geologic timetable, 151–152
  chart, 215
geologists, 4, 108
  use of fossils by, 147, 148, 149
geology, 4
geothermal power, 132
geysers, 200
gibbous moon, 34
glacial lakes, 195
glaciers, 96, 190–192
  advance of, 192
  carrying rocks, 167–168
  carving of land by, 193–195
  continental, 190, 194
  deposition by, 194
  formation of, 191
  meltwater from, 172, 184
  mountain, 191

ice caves, 192
ice crystals
    hailstones starting as, 76
    melting into rain, 75
ice sheets, 190, 194. *See also* continental
    glaciers
igneous rocks, 123–125
    examples of, 124–125
impact craters
    on Callisto, 26
    causes of, 21
    on Mercury, 21
    on Moon, 31
index fossils, 149
Indian Ocean, 144, 171, 173, 176
Indian Plate, 145
infrared waves, 8
inner core, 109
inner planets, 20. *See also* terrestrial
    planets
inorganic, 120
intrusive rocks, 124
Io, 25
ionosphere, 59
irregular galaxies, 12
irrigation, 203
isobars, 68, 117
    used to determine pressure gradient,
    77
isolines, 117

jet streams, 84
Jovian planets, 24–26
    chart, 214
Jupiter, 21, 25–26
    Great Red Spot, 25
    wanderings of, 45

Keck Telescope, 7
kettle lakes, 195

Labrador Current, 179
laccoliths, 124

lakes
    eutrophication of, 205
    glacial, 195
    kettle, 195
    moraine dammed, 195
    oxbow, 188
land breezes, 80
La Niña, 180
lapilli, 139
lateral moraines, 192, 194
latitude, 112–114
    effect on climate of, 94
lava, 4, 123, 183
law of gravity, 30
law of superposition, 148–149
laws of nature, 30
    seat belts and, 31
leap year, 40
lenses, 7
levees, 189
light, 5–6
    energy delivered to Earth in form of, 61
    scattering of, 61
    from stars, distortion of, 8
lightning, 91
light-years, 6–7
lignite, 127
limestone, 126, 167
    caverns, 201
liquids, 63
lithosphere, 135
    hot spots burning holes through, 140
    plates in, 136
Little Dipper, 44
Local Group, 12
local winds, 79–80
    land breezes, 80
    mountain breeze, 81
    produced by mountains and valleys, 81
    sea breezes, 80
    valley breeze, 81
longitude, 112–114
low-pressure centers, 68
    developing along fronts, 88
    winds in, 78

Old Faithful, 200
Oort cloud, 28
optical telescopes, 7
orbit
    of asteroids, 29
    of comets, 27
    of Earth around Sun, 4
    gravitational force and planetary,
        48–49
    of Moon, 30, 32
    of Pluto, 23
orbital period, 28
organic sedimentary rocks, 126–127
Orion, 45
outer core, 109
outwash, 194
    plains, 195
oxbow lakes, 188
oxygen, necessity of, 55
ozone, 59
ozone hole, 59
ozone layer, 59
    thinning, 132

Pacific Ocean, 171, 176, 185
    size of, 172
Pacific Plate, 136, 140
pahoehoe, 139
Pangaea, 133, 134, 145
parallels, 112
peat, 127
penumbra, 35, 36
perigee, 32
perihelion, 40
periods, 151
permeability, 197
pesticides, 204
petrified wood, 148
petroleum, 130–131
phases of Moon, 33
Phobos, 22
photosphere, 18
planetary winds, 82–84
    prevailing winds, 82–83

planets, 17
    defined, 45
    determination of length of year on, 25
    gravitational force and planetary orbit,
        48–49
    outer. See Jovian planets
    terrestrial, 20–23
plate tectonics, 135–137
Pluto, 23
polar air mass, 85, 86
polar front, 88–89
polar highs, 83
Polaris, 41, 44
polarity, 134
polar northeasterlies, 83
polar southeasterlies, 83
polar zone, 94, 95
pollutants, 132, 204
polyconic projections, 115
    topographic maps as, 117
pore spaces, 197
porous rock, 131
precipitation, 75–76
pressure belts, 83
pressure gradient, 77
pressure maps, 67, 117
prevailing westerlies, 83
    air masses brought by, 94
prevailing winds, 4, 82–83
    determining types of air masses, 94
    surface currents created by, 178
prime meridian, 113
primordial soup, 9–10
Proxima Centauri, 7
pulsars, 14
pumice, 124
P waves, 142, 143

quarter moon, 33
quartzite, 129
quasars, 11

radiative zone, 18
radioactive decay, 110

in Northern and Southern
hemispheres, 40–41
wind and pressure belts shifting
with, 83
seat belts, 31
sedimentary rocks, 125–127
chemical, 127
clastic, 126
organic, 126–127
sediments, 186
seismic waves, 142–143
L waves, 142, 143
P waves, 142, 143
S waves, 142, 143
seismographs, 143
seismologists, 143
septic systems, 206
shale, 126, 197
shield cones, 140
Sierra Nevada Mountains, 146
silica, 124
silicates, 109
sills, 124
silt, 189
sink holes, 203
Sirius, 15–16
slate, 128–129
sleet, 75
snout, of glacier, 192
snow, 75, 88, 89
becoming part of glacier, 169
meltwater from, 184
snowflakes, 75, 164
snow line, 191
soil, 167
coarse-grained, 197
solar eclipse, 18, 35–36
solar energy, 60
evaporation of liquid water due to, 168
scattering of, 61
solar flares, 19
solar power, 132
solar prominences, 19

solar system
components of, 17
large gas planets of outer, 21. *See also*
specific planets
Sun, at center of, 20, 39
terrestrial planets of, 20–23
solar wind, 19
solids, 63
solstice, 42
sound waves, 6
South American Plate, 137
Southern Hemisphere, 41
Coriolis effect in, 78
seasons in, 42
South Pole, 40, 41
geographic, 111
latitude of, 112
snow line at, 191
specific gravity, 121
specific heat, 79
specific humidity, 71
speed of light, 6
spiral galaxies, 11–12
spring equinox, 42–43
springs, 184, 198
spring tides, 38
squall line, 90
stalactites, 201
stalagmites, 201
starlight, 8
stars, 13–14. *See also* Sun
absolute magnitude of, 15
Altair, 45
apparent magnitude of, 15
Betelgeuse, 16, 45
binary, 15
birth of, 13
brightness of, 15–16
in constellations, 44
creation of elements in fusion process
of large, 14
Deneb, 45
different kinds of, 14–15
distortion of light from, 8

formation of, 13
lifetime of, 13
Proxima Centauri, 7
Rigel, 45
shooting. *See* meteors
Sirius, 15–16
in Summer Triangle, 45
systems of. *See* galaxies
Vega, 45
stationary front, 88
storms
hurricanes, 92–93
thunderstorms, 90–91
tornadoes, 91–92
stratocumulus clouds, 74
stratosphere, 58–59
stratus clouds, 73
streak, 121
of graphite, 122
streams, 184, 185
runoff from, 172
subduction zones, 137, 175
mountain ranges forming along, 145
ocean trenches occurring along, 176
volcanoes along, 137
sublimation, 164–165
submarine canyons, 175
subpolar lows, 83
subsidence, land, 203
summer, 42
Summer Triangle, 45
summer solstice, 42
Summer Triangle, 45
Sun, 13–14, 15, 17–20. *See also* stars
atmosphere, 18
at center of solar system, 20, 39
chromosphere, 18
convective zone, 18
corona, 18
distance of Earth from, 17
magnetic forces in, 19
nuclear energy produced by, 18
nuclear fusions in, 4, 17
orbit of Earth around, 4, 39–40

photosphere, 18
radiative zone, 18
structure of, 18
sunspot maxima, 19
sunspot minima, 19
sunspots, 19
supernovas, 14
superposition, law of, 148–149
surface currents, 178, 179
surface waves, 142. *See also* L waves
S waves, 142, 143

telescopes, 7–8
Hubble Space Telescope, 7
Keck Telescope, 7
optical, 7
radio, 8
reflecting, 7
refracting, 7
temperate zone, 94, 95
temperature, 65–66
and air pressure, 65–68
change, global, 96
changes with altitude, 57–58
defined, 65
dew-point, 71
and rainfall, six climate controls
affecting, 94
scales, 66
temperature inversion, 75
tephra, 139
terminal moraines, 194–195
terrestrial planets, 20–23. *See also* inner
planets
chart, 213
Earth, 20. *See also* Earth
Mars, 22–23
Mercury, 21–22
Pluto, 23
Venus, 22
thermocline, 173–174
thermometers, 66
thermosphere, 59
thunder, 91

thunderstorms, 88, 90–91
  cold-front, 90
tides, 37–38
till, 194, 195
Titan, 26
Titanic, 179
topographic maps, 117–118
  USGS, 117, 118
tornadoes, 91–92
  safety precautions for, 91
totality, during eclipse, 36
trace fossils, 147
trade winds, 83
transform faults, 136, 142
transpiration, 168–169
tributaries, 185
trilobites, 148
Triton, 26
tropical air mass, 85, 86
tropical depression, 92
tropical storms, 92
tropical zone, 94, 95
Tropic of Cancer, 42
Tropic of Capricorn, 42
troposphere, 58
  convection cells in, 82
  water vapor in, 69
trough, 182
true north, 111
tsunamis, 143
  of 2004, 144
  early warning system for, 144
turbidity currents, 175

ultraviolet waves, 8
umbra, 35, 36
uniform gases, 56
United States Geological Survey (USGS),
  117, 118
universe
  clues in night sky to origin of, 7
  cosmologists and study of, 9–10
  estimating amount of matter in, 10
  primordial soup of, 9

study of, 4
updrafts, 75, 91
  in hurricanes, 93
upwellings, 179–180
uranium-238, 150
uranium dating, 150
Uranus, 21, 26
Ursa Major (Great Bear), 44
Ursa Minor (Little Bear), 44
U-shaped valleys, 194

vacuum
  defined, 63
  of space, 60
valley breeze, 81
valley glaciers, 191
valleys
  production of local winds by, 81
  U-shaped, 194
  V-shaped, 187, 194
variable gases, 56, 62
Vega, 45
vent, 139
Venus, 22
  wanderings of, 45
vertical currents, 178, 179
volcanic eruptions, 4, 138–139
  dust from, causing climate change, 96
  release of volcanic outgassing during,
    56
  on terrestrial planets, 21
  types of, 140–141
  yearly number of, 138
volcanic mountains, 146
volcanic outgassing, 56, 161
volcanoes, 4, 138–141
  activity of, on Io, 25
  along subduction zones, 137
Voyager mission, 25, 26
V-shaped valleys, 187, 194

waning moon, 33
warm front, 87
warm water vents, 174

water
- in atmosphere, 69
- conservation, 203
- different forms of; 163
- effect of gravity on, 185
- elements of, 163
- groundwater as source of drinking, 198
- high specific heat of, 79
- in hydrosphere, 162
- overuse, 202–203
- pollution. *See* water pollution
- running, 184–186
- surface, 184–195

water cycle, 69, 168–169
waterfalls, 188
water pollution, 204–206
- groundwater pollution, 204–205
- ocean water pollution, 205–206
- solutions to problems of, 206
- surface water pollution, 205

water power, 132
watersheds, 185
water table, 198
water vapor, 164
- as heat-trapping greenhouse gas, 69
- in troposphere, 69

wave height, 182
wavelength, 182
waves, 5–6
waxing moon, 33
weather, 65
- and climate, 93–94
- effect of El Niño and La Niña on, 180
- predictions by meteorologists, 68

weather forecasters, 89. *See also* meteorologists
weathering, 126, 129
- chemical, 167

defined, 166
- and erosion, 166–168
- mechanical, 166–167

Wegener, Alfred, 133–134
- use of fossil evidence by, 147

wells, 198
- artesian, 200

Whipple, Fred, 27
white dwarfs, 14
wind, 77–78
- Coriolis effect and, 78
- in hurricanes, 93
- jet streams, 84
- local winds, 79–80
- monsoon winds, 81
- planetary winds, 82–84
- prevailing winds, 4, 82–83
- strength of, 77
- in tornadoes, 92
- trade winds, 83
- wind chill factor, 66–67

wind chill factor, 66
- determining, 67

wind power, 132
wind shear, 91
winter, 42
winter solstice, 42

X rays, 6, 8

year, 40
Yellowstone National Park, 200

zone of aeration, 198
zone of saturation, 198